"HE HIT ME BACK FIRST!"

"HE HIT ME BACK FIRST!"

Creative Visualization Activities
for Parenting and Teaching

EVA D. FUGITT

Jalmar Press
Rolling Hills Estates, California

Published by Jalmar Press
45 Hitching Post Drive, Building 2
Rolling Hills Estates, California 90274

Cover: Judy Ferguson
Typesetting: Patty Graves

IALAC Concept, based on *I Am Loveable and Capable* by Sidney Simon, © 1973, Argus Communications, a division of DLM, Inc., Allen, Texas, used with permission.

LIBK Concept used with permission of Eugene C. Peckham & Associates, Western Training Services, 3849 Long Beach Boulevard, Long Beach, CA 90807. All Rights Reserved.

ISBN: 0-915190-36-2

Library of Congress Catalog Card Number: 82-83063

Printed in the United States of America

Contents

"EVA FUGITT has done a remarkable job in weaving together state of the art imagery and psychosynthesis techniques with learning enhancement procedures so as to accomplish an educational event of real significance. Her book is at once a potent and practical guide for parents and teachers alike in removing learning blocks, evoking self-esteem, and activating the learning potential in every child. That she has done this also with wit and compassion is further testimony to the author's ability to draw forth the possible human in every child."

Jean Houston, Ph.D.
Author of *The Possible Human* and *Life Force: The Psychohistorical Recovery of the Self*

"This is a delightful book. The techniques described are useful and easy to apply, and the general approach is clear, warm, and comprehensive. Educators will find here a unique and needed contribution."

Piero Ferrucci
Author of *What We May Be*

Acknowledgments

It is not easy to write a book. In fact, for me it would have been impossible without the encouragement and support of many special people who contributed to its growth and development. To them I owe enduring gratitude.

To my teacher, Roberto Assagioli, who encouraged me to return to the children, I shall be eternally indebted. He was a teacher in the fullest sense of "educare," able to "call forth" the creative potential within each student. It was he who challenged me to grow in a most unexpected and exciting way.

I would also like to thank my other teachers: Florence Garrigue, Alice Bailey, Edith Stauffer, Piero Ferrucci, Miss Utzinger, Rhonda Davé, and all the teachers who, serving as models, helped me understand my thoughts and experiences. It is with deep appreciation that I acknowledge the response and cooperation I received from my principal, Marvin Tripp, the faculty, parents, and, most importantly, the fourth and fifth graders of Sherman Elementary School. They made it possible.

Thank you to the many psychosynthesists and teachers who so graciously read the manuscript, providing valuable guidance. I wish to acknowledge Hank Maiden, Janette Rainwater, and Bob Williams for their encouragement and advice in helping me find a publisher; Suzanne Mikesell for her patience and willingness to listen, giving careful and clarifying editorial attention; and Ceil Klitgaard, Jan Laughlin, and Pat Miller for proofreading.

A debt of deep gratitude is owed to Ruth Morgan, who held my hand and led me when I would willingly have given up. It was her faith in the work and its need to be given to the children that kept me writing.

I gladly acknowledge my indebtedness and thanks to my sister, Irajoyce Draper, who listened and believed in me. To my children, David, Douglas, and Kathy, who with loving support patiently and humorously endured this process, I give my thanks and love. How do I say thank you to my dear husband, John Fugitt? For his ever-loving patience as I've gone up and down in this seemingly endless writing process, I give my love and gratitude. Thank you, John, for your trust, for encouraging me to begin experiencing my own potential. Thank you for sharing life with me.

Eva D. Fugitt
Santa Clara, California
October, 1982

Preface

In the beginning, I simply wanted to share with a few teachers and parents some of the exciting things that were happening with the children in my classroom. What a surprise to be writing a book! This book has been written in response to the need expressed by many teachers and parents for a practical "how-to" book embracing holistic concepts of living and growing. Its purpose is to meet that need as simply as possible in a way that can be used in both the classroom and the home. The collection of activities is directed toward developing within the child an awareness of his* own inner authority and ability to choose, and the resulting sense of responsibility, freedom, and self-esteem.

The techniques and activities are based on the principles of psychosynthesis, a comprehensive educational approach to human growth and development pioneered in 1911 by Italian psychiatrist Roberto Assagioli. While it is not my intention to include an in-depth study of psychosynthesis, a brief review of its principles will provide a foundation for the activities. Dr. Assagioli's books, *Psychosynthesis* and *The Act of Will,*[1] and Piero Ferrucci's *What We May Be,*[2] are suggested for further study, as are the other books listed in the Bibliography.

Psychosynthesis is a creative approach to the harmonious integration of the whole personality — the physical, emotional, mental, and spiritual aspects of one's self. Utilizing the will, intuition, and creative imagination, psychosynthesis aims to develop within each person an awareness of that deep center which brings these various parts into the unity of wholeness. This awareness is gradually brought into consciousness through a series of techniques, including imagery and visualization, designed to achieve harmony and synthesis within a person and between the person and her surroundings. Psychosynthesis, then, is a process of connecting with the self — the core of our being — so that it can direct our life and relationships with joy and wisdom. For children, I simply say it is getting in touch with the "Wise Part" within us.

This rather complex definition proved difficult for many parents and teachers. I simplified it by saying that psyche means self and synthesis means putting it all together, or "getting your act together." They were comfortable with this definition, being more interested in the activities and results than in the theory.

---

*While I support the need to be all-inclusive, I find the use of "he/she," "s/he," and "he or she" cumbersome in writing. For the sake of simplicity I alternate between the masculine and feminine pronouns wherever appropriate.

The psychosynthesis used with children is highly modified from that used in adult counseling. Dr. Assagioli's basic techniques of creative imagination, dis-identification, and development of will have been adapted to a child's level of growth. The concepts of awareness introduced at this level are that children have many unique and varied parts to themselves, that they have a unifying center or "Wise Part" within that they can trust, and that they control their own thoughts and behavior through the implementation of the will.

A distinctive characteristic of psychosynthesis is its emphasis on the *will* as an essential function of the self and as the source of all choices and decisions. Will includes deliberation, motivation, decision, affirmation, planning, and execution. To be well-balanced, the will must be wise, strong, and good.

Piero Ferrucci, an associate of Dr. Assagioli and author of *What We May Be*, says: "We can truly and freely choose, bearing the full responsibility of self-determination. It is to this evolutionary acquisition, still very much in development, that we give here the name of will." Ferrucci continues, "(T)he will in its true essence can explain a host of human attainments, while its absence can account for legions of psychological disturbances. If understood in its proper perspective, the will is, more than any other factor, the key to human freedom and personal power."[3]

In psychosynthesis, the will is consciously developed through a variety of techniques. One simple technique is the use of "I will" statements. In contrast to the negative "I won't" forms which block action ("I won't make a lot of noise"), "I will" statements invoke the will to act ("I will be quiet"). Imagining what could be, children create their own solutions to problems. Another technique for strengthening the will is that of setting goals. Children select one specific personal goal *of their own choosing* to be achieved each day, list benefits of achieving and burdens of not achieving it, make specific plans for achieving it, and evaluate their progress. This technique develops logical, sequential thinking that takes disciplined use of the will.

The use of imagery is basic to psychosynthesis. All the activities — which include discussions, role playing, drama, art, creative writing, personal journals, and the setting of personal goals — make extensive use of the creative imagination to build self-awareness, self-concept, and awareness of choice.

This book is the result of a two-year research project using these methods in the elementary classroom. A summary of the research project can be found in the Appendix. The results of the project for treatment and control groups, including pre- and post-testing for academic achievement and growth of self-esteem, are discussed.

The activities presented are not just for the troubled child who creates disturbances but for children of all ages, all levels of intelligence, and all abilities. Students behaving "well," — that is, not causing "trouble" — still need the basic how-to's for developing their inner authority, understanding how to make choices, and accepting responsibility for the results of those choices.

The book includes original activities created for the project as well as some adapted from Dr. Assagioli's techniques for adult therapy. The criterion of inclusion was simply whether or not the activity has worked to nourish within the child an awareness of the self and of his ability to control his own thoughts and behavior.

The order of the activities reflects a transition from easiest to most difficult. At the beginning of each activity, its purpose and its relationship to the concepts of psychosynthesis are briefly explained. Required materials are specified and comments on my experience with the exercise follow each procedure.

From the project's last class, two students were placed in a class for the gifted and one in a special art class. The children with severe behavioral problems made good progress both academically and socially. However, the children who were basically "all right" — behaving within so-called acceptable norms — made quantum leaps in their progress. As these students discovered and honored their inner authority, a sense of excitement emerged. A willingness to learn developed as the discovery that they had choices gave a sense of freedom and joy to their learning process.

Use these lessons as guidelines, as stepping stones to your own unique creativity. They are an attempt to bring the affective and cognitive domains into balance within the classroom and at home. They are simple, but not easy. They will become easy as your own synthesis evolves.

All of us have memories of a special person, perhaps a teacher, who stands above others as having helped us at a special time of need. Such a teacher in my life was Miss Utzinger, my high school geometry teacher. She was a plain, "no-nonsense" type of teacher but gentle and fair. One day while staying after class for help I commented on her patience. She responded with words that made an indelible impression on me: "Once upon a time I didn't know either."

In the beginning it is hard. There is resistance. First learning to tie your shoe is hard. First learning to change from manuscript to cursive writing is hard. First learning to read is hard. As teachers and parents, we value these skills and teach them regardless of resistance. It is the same with learning the skills of self-correction.

A word of caution. With any system of techniques, no matter how high the ideal, there is always the possibility of misuse, of manipulation. Continually assess your purpose for using these techniques. A teacher is one who helps a person discover what is already in him, not a "shaper of persons into prearranged forms. . . ."[5] You have a unique place in the life of each child. Be authentic. Teach with sensitivity and humanness. You must work out for yourself the kind of relationship that will help the child as well as yourself be more honest and more genuine.[6] When you have within yourself the right attitudes and skills, you have the potential to "call forth" (educare) the creative potential within each child, to change a direction of self-destructiveness to one of self-fulfillment.

Though this book was written initially for classroom use, so many parents have responded that I want to give special encouragement to them. All the principles and exercises presented can be used with individuals as well as with groups, in the home as well as in the classroom. Home encounters are, of course, an even greater force than school encounters in shaping the child's ability to handle life creatively. As a parent you, too, are an educator. Trust your own process, trust that "Wise Part" within you as well as within the child. Use your creative imagination, blending your love and will into a gift of choice and responsibility for your children.

A discussion of "burdens and benefits" as presented in the section on goals could take place around the dinner table. Parents and children can share their personal feelings of what a burden or benefit is to them, beginning the gradual process of building a common vocabulary for self-correction. Many of the activities — journal writing, guided imagery, etc. — can be adapted for family nights at home. As in the classroom, it is important to introduce the concepts in a relaxed, supportive environment rather than in a time of crisis.

Above all, remember always that once upon a time I-you-we didn't know either. And so we learn together, little by little by little.

FOOTNOTES

1. Roberto Assagioli, M.D., *Psychosynthesis* (New York: Viking Press, 1965); and *The Act of Will* (New York: Viking Press, 1973).

2. Piero Ferrucci, *What We May Be* (Los Angeles: J. P. Tarcher, Inc., 1982).

3. *Ibid.*, p. 73

4. *Ibid.*, p. 72.

5. Louis J. Rubin, *Facts and Feelings in the Classroom* (New York: Walker & Co., 1973), p. 153.

6. Clark Moustakas, *The Authentic Teacher* (Cambridge, Mass.: Howard A. Doyle Publishing Co., 1972), p. 259.

DEDICATED

to

Milly Collinsworth and Viola Davis

and

to all teachers and students who seek to be co-learners in the process of living full, creative lives of joy and service.

Introduction
The Search for a Better Way

The children came running into the room, jumping on chairs, walking across desks, yelling and laughing, totally disregarding me and the teacher's aide. Upon seeing me, one little boy shouted, "A substitute!" He ran outside and proceeded to run around and around the portable all morning, yelling and throwing orange and banana peels through the windows. Whenever the aide or I would try to stop him, he would run out a nearby gate and down the sidewalk.

The aide walked quietly around the room. Stopping and putting her arm around a child, she would whisper, "Now, you'll be good, won't you? For me, please?" Although the children simply shrugged and ignored her, she continued to sweetly love them.

I, on the other hand, had become the strong-willed, external authoritarian, yelling and demanding cooperation. These were seven-year-olds, almost at the end of second grade! One expects children to have learned some form of discipline by this time. I physically placed some children in their seats and dared them to move.

The class was "way out in the south forty" of an elementary school in the ghetto of a metropolitan city. On arriving that morning, I found no lesson plans and the room in a total chaos of unorganized papers and materials. The only thing on the bulletin board was an old spelling test dated September. I thought to myself, "What is this teacher doing? There is no caring here!"

By the time the ten o'clock recess came, I was closer to walking out than I ever had been in my entire teaching career. I was not an inexperienced teacher; I had taught school in the affluent suburbs, in the "poor white" section of east Los Angeles, and on an Indian reservation. I went to the office and asked for help. This was an extremely large school with a large support staff. The principal was away at a conference and the rest of the staff were at "an important meeting downtown." The secretary said, "That's the way all the kids are here. There's nothing much you can do about it."

I returned to the room with a great sense of anger at the administration for not providing help and of frustration with myself for not having greater skills. I also felt impatient with the sweet little assistant (I later discovered she was not an aide but a credentialed teacher), who kept saying, "Just love them, the poor dears. You have to remember where they come from." I simply could not accept that. To me, it was plain do-gooder prejudice.

I had yard duty at the eleven o'clock recess. Boys were swinging empty coke bottles over their heads and throwing them, splattering broken glass on the blacktop. The other teacher on yard duty shrugged and said, "You'll get used to it. They really aren't bad."

By then I was determined that my class would learn at least one thing before they went home. By lunchtime they were actually staying in their seats, had completed one math assignment, and had listened to a story. The assistant teacher told me later that they had been "so good today, much better than usual!"

I was exhausted. I knew there had to be a better way than the strong, externally imposed authority I had used or the weak, misdirected love of the assistant teacher. These children deserved good teaching! But what was that "better way"?

An incident occurred a few days later while I was substituting in another school — an incident that made a lasting impression on me and deepened forever my commitment to developing a "better way" of working with children.

I had the children in the library when two boys got into an argument over a comb and started to physically battle it out. The class went wild, jumping up and down, yelling whooooeeee!! I had caught the two boys by the arms and had them on either side of me, each straining to reach the other, when the door to the next classroom opened. A teacher stood quietly in the doorway and said, "May I help you?" I looked at him. The children looked at him. Silence. A respectful silence. The man was of slight stature, plain in appearance, and had a slight limp. He also had a quiet presence that penetrated us all. He asked what the problem was and listened quietly and fully. He then placed a gentle hand on one boy's shoulder and suggested that he "come with me for awhile." The class quietly returned to work.

At lunchtime I sought out that man and what a time of sharing we had! He was a dedicated teacher who firmly loved the children. He evoked a disciplined response from them without resorting to "rule with an iron hand" or "just love them, the poor dears."

Three teachers, three approaches to discipline. One using love without will, evoking disrespect and non-cooperation. The second (myself) using will without love, evoking cooperation with resentment. The third creatively using love with will, evoking trust and growth.

I left that day determined to discover and develop within myself that same inner presence that radiated love and will, gentleness and firmness, and loving strength.

A few months later I was assigned to a school as a full-time teacher with my own class of fourth graders. These children were in an elementary school of a large inner-city school district in California's San Francisco Bay Area. Ninety-five percent of the students were black and the remaining five percent Asian, Caucasian, Chicano, and Native American. Because students' math, reading, and language scores on the Comprehensive Test of Basic Skills (CTBS) were below the 50th percentile, the school was part of the Compensatory Education program funded by California's Senate Bill 90.

2

The following statements about the children in my classroom were given to me by parents, foster parents, and social workers:

"An incorrigible discipline problem."
"Aggressive and undisciplined."
"Constant fighting and use of obscenity."
"A foster child. Mother in an institution and father an alcoholic. Three brothers in jail, one in San Quentin."
"When she was five years old she saw her father kill her mother, whom he found in bed with a lover."

How does a classroom teacher help children with such problems? Children who, because of life experiences, have a low sense of self-esteem and little awareness of how to correct their behavior? Children who, in order to survive, are behaving the only way they know how. . .?

I continued to search for alternative ways to give concrete, practical help to the children and for a greater sense of purpose and direction in teaching based on that radiating sense of "knowing who I am."

In this process, I discovered that I placed many demands on myself, on the children, and on the educational system. Some of the heaviest demands were that I "be the perfect teacher" (the teacher-God complex!) and that the children "be the perfect students."

It was difficult and even painful for me to learn that I could not be "responsible" for the behavior of my students. Each student ultimately makes his own choice of response, even within a limited environment. I was setting myself up for failure. That demand created a tension within me that absorbed a great deal of my attention and energy, thus limiting my creativity and my ability to see problems in a larger perspective. Such demands for perfection placed both me and the students in a closed box, allowing no room for creative choices. There was no way I could "make" a child learn to multiply, learn to read, learn to "be good" unless the child's awareness at the time permitted her to choose to do these things. However, I could be responsible for my own behavior. I could be responsible for creating an environment that motivates, challenges, and invites a disciplined, creative response to learning.

I began to trust the inner wisdom of the child to teach himself. I began to trust the teaching of others along the child's way, to trust the life process itself to teach the child. . . and to teach me. I no longer had to demand that every child learn in the way I thought she "should." As these demands were released I experienced a deeper sense of freedom and creativity than I'd ever experienced before.

My feelings of freedom and awareness of choice contrasted sharply with the lack of awareness exhibited by the children. They were unaware that they, too, had choices and an inner wisdom they could draw upon to guide their daily actions. Children today are caught in a confusion of choices: they are confronted with the most fundamental questions of values and purpose: "How do I choose? "By whose authority do I choose?" "What happens when I choose?" Such choices are frightening, for they require the child in a sense to create his own identity.

Parents and teachers also are caught in this confusion of choices, especially in regard to discipline and the use of will. This confusion is illustrated by the story of a family who left their fifteen-year-old daughter with friends while they went out of town for the weekend. The parents had made earlier arrangements with the friends, but failed to check with them before leaving town. In the meantime, the daughter had spread the word around school that her parents would be gone, so "Come to my house for a party."

Fifty to sixty teenagers showed up, proceeded to get drunk on liquor from the family's well-stocked cabinet and "trashed" the house, throwing furniture into the swimming pool, using spray paint on the rugs, knocking holes in walls, and breaking valuable art objects.

Shocked and angry on their return, the parents imposed severe restrictions on their daughter. Other parents objected that they were too strict, while a few supported the restrictions. Since this behavior wasn't new to the community, a group of parents, teachers, and school administrators met. Once again, there was the conflict between the non-interfering, "do-your-own-thing" approach and the severe, externally imposed authoritarian approach. Once again, confusion had led to two extremes of discipline: permissiveness and authoritarianism. Each is used with good intent but with poor results.

CHOICE

Because of the misunderstanding that discipline and will repressed creativity and spontaneity, the use of the will has been on the back burner in recent times. Today, as the stories above illustrate, there is an attempt to reinstate its use as a positive force in our lives. In the desire to help children learn responsibility for behavior, both parents and teachers are offering more structured forms of discipline that firmly present the consequences of choices.

However, we must be careful not to confuse real will with Victorian willpower, warns Ferrucci. "The fact that many people have been calling 'will' what was actually stern self-restraint should not tempt us to throw out the baby of true will with the bathwater of Victorian self-denial." Ferrucci gives us this encouraging statement: "We can clear up this misunderstanding as soon as we realize that *the real function of the will is to direct, not to impose.*"[1]

To direct, not to impose. A powerful concept, but difficult to manifest. Is it possible to teach a child to direct his own will without imposing?

Assagioli, founder of psychosynthesis, suggests four stages through which one may achieve freedom, self-realization, and right relationships with others:[2]

1) gaining knowledge of one's personality

2) achieving control of its various elements

3) realizing one's true self — the discovery or creation of a unifying center

4) achieving psychosynthesis — the formation or reconstruction of the personality around the new center.

The third stage, realization of one's true self, arises from the experience of self-control that comes from making choices. If we do not have the opportunity to make choices, we are unable to experience our own will (the source of all choices) or realize our true self. Through experiencing the consequences of our choices, we come to see who we really are.

When choices are externally imposed, as in the examples of the authoritarian approach to discipline, they no longer remain free choices. Instead of nourishing the self, they evoke adaptive behavior based on fear or rebellious behavior based on resentment. When imposed choices are the only ones offered, the child becomes dependent on outside authorities for the determination of his values. While the imposed will may serve as a model for a short time, its beneficial effects do not last. If an externally imposed will is the *only* language a child understands, then we must speak in that language *while* we are in the process of teaching the new language — one of self-correction.

Ferrucci, too, warns of the problems that may arise without the experience of choice. When the individual will is not recognized or developed (as in the "just love them" approach to discipline) or "is violated in a consistent and enduring way. . .pain and illness arise. And, because the will is the faculty closest to our self, when it is infringed upon the hurt goes all the way to the core."[3] When this happens it can have fearful consequences for the self and for society as a whole.

It is the real will, then, that must be challenged, channeled, and brought forth into service if the child is to learn to make choices that will nurture self-esteem, enhance the process of self-discipline, and lead to the fulfillment of his inner potential.

In psychosynthesis, the will is consciously developed through a wide variety of techniques. I realized that these techniques applied not only to my own growth but also to the problems of my students. Here was a way to help the children learn how to consciously choose what they will do and how they will do it, and to be aware of the consequences of their choices. Directing, not imposing. Balancing love and will.

One of the basic purposes of psychosynthesis is to release the energy of the self, allowing it to become more and more a source of inner guidance, strength, wisdom, joy, love, and purpose. Recognition of the "Wise Part" within or unifying center is developed as a tool or guide for making the best possible choices we are capable of making. It is by bringing forth our highest qualities that these techniques help us to solve our everyday problems and to function in the world more serenely and effectively, with a sense of dignity and respect.

LITTLE BY LITTLE

High ideals! But in the ghetto?? How do we bring these ideals down into the nitty-gritty of the everyday life of children? How can such ideals be taught in the demanding schedule of the classroom? Is it possible to present to children the principles of relaxation, visualization, and the use of the will? Are they capable of learning these concepts?

Questions, questions, questions as I searched for ways of meeting the children's needs. Will it work? Will it work for deprived, underprivileged children who test two or more years below grade level? Children who are almost totally dependent on an external form of authority, having little awareness that they have choices in their response to life? How is the will evoked within the child? Can I trust the process of evocation? What happens if I trust my own inner wisdom and release my dependence on external authority? Do I dare try psychosynthesis activities with a class of thirty-two fourth graders in an inner-city school?

As my own synthesis evolved, I became more and more convinced that the principles of psychosynthesis are ageless, raceless, and sexless. I also came to believe strongly that these principles of interpersonal relationships must be taught to children — that we cannot wait until they become adults requiring in-depth therapy involving countless hours, expense, and heartaches.

The experiment began, for survival's sake if nothing else. I could no longer continue using the strong, external authority method. The permissive love method was simply not suitable to my personality. Hesitant, fearful, eager, committed, I began, little by little by little.

Listen to the words, "little by little by little." This beautiful, energy-releasing phrase was given to me by a man I met while teaching a workshop in Copenhagen, Denmark. Deep in a philosophical discussion of life, he would say, "Remember, little by little by little." Each time he would say this I would experience a deepening sense of trust, a letting go of an internal demand that I, and everything else, "be perfect." Once again, I would realize the joy of trusting the teaching-learning-growing process.

As in all learning, success bred confidence until eventually the principles of psychosynthesis were a natural and integral part of the daily lesson plans. I am firmly committed to teaching the basic skills — the "onesies and twosies" of the three "R's." However, it wasn't too long before I realized that I had added a fourth "R" to the curriculum: that of Right Relations. As the ideas took concrete form, the children's social and academic behavior also took on a different form, one of creative cooperation with the learning process. A bonding of teacher-student relationships was experienced in our classroom. Teaching and learning became an exciting adventure. Parents began responding with enthusiasm, teachers began asking questions, and I began presenting workshops.

I hope that these methods will serve you, your students, and your children as you, too, discover that inner authority allowing you to live fully and creatively. Trust your own process, the process that calls forth love and will and the understanding of when to push and when to release, all in right proportion. The process is not always easy. It is not always gentle. It is not always rough. As with all tools, when used with the right attitude the exercises in this book can create and transform, proceeding little by little by little.

FOOTNOTES

1. Piero Ferrucci, *What We May Be* (Los Angeles: J. P. Tarcher, Inc., 1982), p. 77.

2. Roberto Assagioli, *Psychosynthesis* (New York: Viking Press, 1965), p. 21.

3. Ferruci, *op. cit.,* p. 74.

Activities

Will — Choice

WILL EXERCISES

AREA: Self-discipline, concentration, focus, determination

COMMENT: These exercises are designed to encourage the act of concentration and the development of the will. They provide an excellent opportunity to assess a child's ability to concentrate on simple activities and give direction in planning the needed developmental skills.

MEDIA: A covered tray of ten or twelve objects such as a paper clip, rubber band, comb, bottle top, coin, etc. Pencil and paper. Paper or cloth bag.

PROCEDURE:

Exercise one: Small group

Have the children gather around the covered tray with paper and pencil available. Explain that they will have a given amount of time (determined by adult's assessment of their needs) to *silently* look at the objects, remembering as many of them as possible. When the time is up the objects will be covered and they will list as many as they can remember, again in a given amount of time. If they do no know the name of the object or cannot write it, they may draw a picture of it. Remind them to do it silently, as this helps them to concentrate.

Exercise two: Large or small group

Direct the children to perform a variety of seemingly useless tasks with their body by first saying the words, "I will . . ." before each task. Have the children repeat after you the "I will. . ." statement before performing.

1. "I will tap the pencil ten times. 1, 2, 3. . . ." (count out loud).
2. "I will clap my hand five times. 1, 2, 3. . ."
3. "I will stand on one foot for six counts. 1, 2, 3. . ."
4. "I will pat my head with my left hand for 8 counts."
5. "I will. . ." Teacher uses creative imagination.

The ability to focus on one activity may be so lacking that a child will be able to tap the pencil only three times before he is distracted. Saying the words, "I will. . ." at the beginning of each statement is important to evoking the conscious use of will. These activities are comfortable and enjoyable to the children. Simple exercises such as these are as unlimited as the teacher's creative imagination and act of will.

Exercise three: Individually or small group.

Using a bag containing several objects of various shapes, sizes, and texture, direct the child to place his hands in the bag and, silently and without looking, feel the objects in the bag. Say to the child: "Feel the shape of the object. Be aware of its size. What does the surface feel like? (texture). When you are ready you may write the names of the objects, draw the objects or tell me about them."

OBSERVATION: These are simple, familiar exercises used for the development of a variety of skills. The conscious use of them for calling forth the will gives an added dimension. Many children are not able to concentrate long enough to even do these simple exercises. When they do, it can be done with a sense of achievement.

I WILL STATEMENTS

AREA: Self-discipline and use of will

COMMENT: The "I will" statement is designed to reinforce the positive aspect of self-correction. How often a child is taught what not to do rather than what to do ("Don't run in the hall" rather than "Walk in the hall" or "Don't be late" rather than "Be on time").

MEDIA: Paper and pencil.

PROCEDURE: Both the adult and the child use the positive "I will. . ." when correcting as opposed to the negative, "Don't" and "I won't. . ."

Have the child write a plan of behavior as part of the process of self-correcting and accepting responsibility for the behavior. He is to write a statement of what he *will do* to correct the present situation or the next time he is in such a situation.

OBSERVATION: Over an eight-year period of teaching this seemingly simple concept, I found it to be quite difficult not only for children but also for teachers to change the negative pattern of "I won't. . ." to a positive "I will." It takes a conscious act of will to change a well-established thoughtform.

When a child says, "I won't do it anymore. . ." guide the awareness of choice by asking, "What will you do?" Usually he'll repeat, "I won't never, never do it again." Again say, "If you aren't going to do it, what *will* you do?" Continue asking in such a way as to evoke an "I will" statement such as, "I will listen." "I will read." "I will wait for my turn." etc.

This is a simple activity but not easy. It involves focused use of will, and there will be resistance *in both children and adults.* Our language is so full of shoulds, oughts, and nots. I hear myself saying, "Should is a word we shouldn't have." Internally I interrupt myself, rephrase, and say, "It would be better to have something else." This gives power, freedom, open-endedness and evokes creativity, taking us to the next step. Shoulds, oughts and nots stifle creativity. The need for limitations or a framework is still there. However, to state the need for a change in a positive way, without the should, ought or not, allows for growth and new ways of thinking.

G.

Dear Mother,
          I was having a feet fight with
my ~~mates~~ at listening time. I will keep my feet to my self
~~I forgot my books and I will bring them back tomorrow~~

W.

Dear Mother I
Was lating sunflower seeds
in the Class room
My plan is to lat
at lunch time

C.

I was walking very slow and
the traffic girls told me to hurry
up but I wound't

My Plan is to be on the
Jiffy.

MY GOAL
Benefits and Burdens

AREA: Self evaluation, self-discipline, act of will

COMMENT: This activity offers an opportunity to use the will in an act of concentration. It introduces children to the experience of making a choice through using the will in the act of deliberation, decision, affirmation, planning, direction of the execution and evaluation. It develops self awareness and self-discipline and has potential of enhancing self-esteem. It involves planning. Plans and goals give a much needed lift to life, and people with many plans tend to be zestful and purposeful.

MEDIA: Goal chart, goal sheet, pencil, group discussion.

PROCEDURE: Introduce subject by having a general discussion with children seated in an informal circle. Discuss general class goals such as a class goal in reading, math, or athletic goals. Use as many examples as needed to clarify definition of a goal.

Discuss with the children the meaning of words, *benefits* and *burdens*. Benefits are the results or consequences of achieving the goal. Burdens are the results or consequences of not achieving the goal. This process is extremely important as these two words will be used and referred to over and over. They will become important tools in supporting self-correction. The concepts include feelings and attitudes as well as tangible results.

Following the discussion have the children write examples of benefits and burdens. These may be done at different times. It is important that there is a good understanding of what a goal is and what benefits and burdens are before personal goals are worked on.

Allow three to five sessions of general discussion before introducing the individual goal sheet to ensure a firm basis for future work. In the beginning this is a difficult activity as it takes strong mental discipline. The teacher needs to work directly with the class the first several days of writing the individual goal, giving examples, stressing that only *one simple* goal is chosen. To be effective the goal must be very *specific*, such as: 10 math problems, or do my homework at 4:30 pm, or run around the track 15 times. Specific goals help to develop the skill to focus. General goals can be too vague and are less effective in developing the use of will. In the beginning choose a goal that can be achieved fairly easily, such as:

My goal for today is to sharpen my pencil when I first come into the room.

Benefits: I will have a sharp pencil for my work.
I will not have to disturb the class.
I will feel good about having a sharp pencil.
My writing will be neater with a sharp pencil.

Burdens: My pencil will be broken.
I will have to disturb the class to sharpen it.
I will be slow in getting started with my work.
I will feel bad and probably get mad.

The object is to work on something that is at first very simple and easy to achieve, while developing the awareness of choice, benefits, burdens and planning. The goal may be on any subject the child chooses, academic, playground, friends, home. One child had a goal to make a new friend and did!

For one child the goal may be to finish one math problem; for another it may be to finish a book and write a report on it for the day. After the children have had several days of writing the individual goals with the adult's guidance, a booklet with a month's supply of goal sheets may be given to each child. An effective way is to have the children write their goal each morning upon first entering the classroom. At that time evaluation of the previous day's goal may be done. This avoids the hassle of remembering to do it again at the close of the day, though of course this would be ideal if the schedule permitted.

Emphasize that the goal sheets will not be graded. Though this exercise certainly uses language skills it is not be be used as a "language lesson." Children are always greatly relieved when the stress of grading is removed. Evaluation is based on the child's growing awareness that he/she has a choice of behavior, a choice of possible consequences, a choice in planning. An awareness of choice evokes the act of will.

The use of the goal exercise not only helps the child to gain awareness of choice and responsibility but helps to develop organized, sequential, logical thinking, concentration, and follow-through. In the beginning a student will often have a goal to finish math and a benefit of getting one hundred in spelling. A logical connection between goal, benefit, and burden has to be established.

Not only does the student benefit but the parent or teacher benefits in learning where the child's needs are, what is relevant to the child and what areas need developing. For instance, the goal to "be nice" gives an excellent springboard for a discussion on values clarification. Ask such questions as:

"What does 'be nice' mean?"

"How do you be 'nice'?"

"Can you be 'nice' when you are angry?"

"Do you have to do something with your anger before you can be nice?"

"What are some of the things you can do with your anger that won't hurt someone or something?"

OBSERVATION: Kim* arrived new to class just about the time the goals exercise was introduced in the spring semester. She was a very lonely, shy girl — thin, malnourished, with long, stringy, unwashed blond hair, and big blue eyes sunk in a bony face. She looked terribly lost as the only white child in an inner-city class of all black children.

When the goal booklets were finished after about 4-6 weeks the students were no longer required to make daily goals. Kim asked if she could continue doing hers. At the end of the year she proudly came to me with a huge stack of goal sheets in her hand, eyes sparkling and saying, "I won all my goals except three!" By that time she had made friends and was an eager student and, most exciting of all, she was eager for life — self-confidence and happiness radiated from her. Her reading level had increased 1.6 (1

---

*Names of all children have been changed.

year, 6 months) in the four months she was in the class. When writing the year-end report in the cumulative record I was stunned to read in the previous year's report that Kim was an "incorrigible discipline problem" and was working far below grade level. Kim continued to blossom in the next year, accepting responsibility for her choices with confidence.

A high school counselor found the goal sheet to be an excellent tool for self-correction. He had students who were sent to him with behavior problems select one specific goal for a given time, i.e., choice of behavior for the next 15 minutes or one activity for one class. (Building self-discipline uses *one* step at a time.)

A high school home economics teacher used a combination of creative imagination, visualization, and the goal sheet for highly effective results in a sewing class.

MY GOAL

My goal for today is to _do test 32_ comfortably.

Benefits:

1. I will be happy
2. I will be proud
3. I will be able to finish Unit III faster
4. I will have my name on the Math Chart sooner.

Burdens:

1. I will be mad.
2. I will not be proud.
3. I will have to do it toumarro.
4. I will not have my name on the Chart sooner.

Plans to achieve it:

1. Stay after school and get the test
2. Do my Homework.
3. Do it from 6:30 to 7:00 at night

Evaluation:

1. Did I win? Yes Why: I followed my plan.

2. Did I lose: No Why: I followered my plan

MY GOAL

My goal for today is to _go into the library_ comfortably.
and self 5 books!

Benefits:

1. _I did help Mrs. D._
2. _Mrs. Grambam will be happy at me._
3. _I will be proud!_
4. _There will not be so much books._

Burdens:

1. _I don't help Mrs. D._
2. _Mrs. Graham will be mad._
3. _I will be mad at my self._
4. _There will to much books_

Plans to achieve it:

1. _Remember to go to the libary._
2. _Do it at 10:00 to 10:10._
3. _Do it comfortabldy._

Evaluation:

1. Did I win? _Yes_ Why: _I followed my plan_

2. Did I lose? _No_ Why? _I followed my plan_

MY GOAL

My goal for today is to _make a hit at P.E._ comfortably.

Benefits:

1. _I will feel proud._
2. _I will have two hits_
3. _I will be able to be picked first._
4. _I will not have to practice so much_

Burdens:

1. _I will feel uncapable._
2. _I will have one home run_
3. _I will be picked last._
4. _I will have to practice hard._

Plans to achieve it:

1. _Don't run to school and get tired._
2. _Eat a good breakfast._
3. _Practice today after doing my homework_

Evaluation:

1. Did I win? _Yes_ Why? _I followed my plan._

2. Did I lose? _No_ Why? _I followed my plan_

THE MAGIC QUESTION
"How Does That Help You?"

AREA: Self-discipline, self-awareness and act of will

COMMENT: The question, "How does that help you?" is designed to help children recognize and take responsibility for their behavior. It evokes the innate need for self fulfillment that lies deep within each child, breaking through the usual defenses. The adult is not the authority at that moment. The child is permitted to contact his own authority, to participate in the process of thinking, consciously choosing a behavioral response.

PROCEDURE: When a child is behaving in such a way as to disturb his own or class progress, quietly ask, "Tommy, how does that help you? You needn't answer, but just quietly go inside yourself and think about it."

OBSERVATION: Invariably when asked in this way the child will stop, think a moment and correct the behavior. Usually nothing else need be said unless the parent or teacher wishes to acknowledge the changed behavior with a smile or a thank you or some other appropriate remark.

I am continually amazed at the strength of this question. It has never failed to evoke some form of self-correction. I call it the magic question. Teachers often ask, "What if there is a negative response?" I can only answer that as long as I've used it, there has never been a negative response. However, it needs to be asked in a nonjudgmental tone and, like everything else, it can be overused and lose its magic. There is usually a silent response with a change of behavior, e.g., a child with a disruptive behavior may simply sit in silence for the rest of the period, or choose an appropriate action such as finishing a math assignment.

To expand individual awareness to group awareness the question may change to, "How is that helping the group?" or, "How is that helping your neighbor?"

One fourth grader who had been exposed to this question went on to the fifth grade still in need of much growth in self-discipline. Shortly after the beginning of the year the fifth grade teacher came to me and asked what he could do with Charlene. Her behavior was "driving him up the wall." It was suggested that the next time her behavior was disturbing he might ask, "How is that helping you, Charlene?" He later reported that he didn't know what happened, but it worked like a charm. When asked, she stopped, looked at him, thought for a moment, smiled and quietly went back to her desk and sat down. Though still dependent on external control for behavior modification, at that moment she was able to stop and correct the behavior with an internal decision.

QUESTION SUGGESTIONS
Class Meetings

AREA: Value clarification, choice, self-correction, act of will

COMMENT: These questions are designed to evoke from the child awareness of 1) behavior patterns, 2) a particular mind set, and 3) the choice of self-correction. Alternatives of choice are expressed, expanding the limitation of perceived choices.

MEDIA: Class meetings, small or large groups.

PROCEDURE: Children sit in a circle. Have a large card with the words MY TURN on it. As the question is asked, pass the card to the person next to you. The child answers and passes the card to his/her neighbor. They can speak only if they have the card. This is an excellent technique with which to begin a discussion. It not only helps control the discussion, but gives everyone an opportunity to speak. If a child doesn't wish to speak she/he may say, "I pass." Many quiet ones will speak if they don't have to "fight for the floor." The talkative children also are given the opportunity to learn sharing and listening skills. As the discussion evolves, the card can be set aside.

Ask questions that evoke answers from within the child, calling forth his/her own authority to see cause and effect in relationships and situations. Set aside all judgment, moralizing, imposition of values. When the environment is free of judgment and when friendliness and acceptance are present, the discussion is open, creative and receptive to growth.

Give the first question. When several have answered and it seems comfortable, move on to the next question.

Introductory Statement: I often hear boys and girls say, "I'll be nice."
1. What does "be nice" mean?
2. How do you "be nice?"
3. How do you know it's nice?
4. Who tells you so?
5. What does "being nice" feel like?
6. Can you "be nice" when you are angry?
7. What happens if you try to "be nice" when you are angry?
8. Do you have to do something with the anger (or hurt, or jealousy, or. . .) before you can "be nice"?
9. What are some of the things you can do with the anger that won't hurt yourself, someone else or some thing?

Be specific, specific, specific. This is difficult. The mind will resist. The act of will is involved. It is much easier to generalize. Let the child think! Call forth the wisdom within the child. Honor his knowledge.

Introductory Statement: We often hear people say, "I'll get into trouble."
1. What does trouble mean?
2. How do you know it's trouble?
3. Is getting "into trouble" the same for you as it is for_____?
4. Is "in trouble" different for different people?
5. What does "in trouble" feel like?
6. Give a specific act that means "getting into trouble" for you, e.g., I'll get a spanking, I can't watch T.V., I'll have to stay after school. (Evoke awareness of a specific consequence for a specific behavior.)

Introductory Statement: I hear there's going to be a big fight after school. What happens if there is a fight?
(The usual response is, "There'll be trouble—BIG—trouble!")
1. What kind of trouble?
   "Get sent to the office."
2. What happens there?
   "Call my mom. . ."
3. Then what will happen?
   "Man, I get in trouble! I mean TROUBLE!"
4. What kind of trouble?

Continue evoking answers from the children. Set aside judgment, moralizing, preaching, etc. Be as objective as possible.

5. If there is a fight are you willing to accept the burdens? You have the choice.
6. What alternatives do you have?
7. How would you like it to happen?

OBSERVATION: These periods of sharing offer again the possibility of alternatives of choice, responsibility for choice, and consequences of choice. They provide an opportunity for choice to come from the internal authority as opposed to an external authority, evoking self-correction.

Many a fight was prevented by such a discussion. One day the discussion became quite heated. Reggie stood very close to me, stuck out his chin and asked with voice full of frustration and eyes pleading, "What'cha gonna do if someone wants to fight ya and ya don't want to and ya don't want to get in trouble, but they call ya coward and sissy! They keep pickin' on ya! What'cha gonna do? Huh? Huh?"

I stood there quietly looking at him, seeing the hint of tears, hearing the age-old question — how to handle the bully. With a sadness in my heart I answered, "Reggie, I don't have an answer. I wish I did. It is an answer that each person must find for himself. Adults still ask the same question. Countries are at war because of that question. It is not an easy question to answer. I can only say that you do have a choice. If you do or do not fight, you must be willing to accept the burdens or benefits of your choice. Sometimes you may choose to fight. That's all right. It is your choice, your burden or benefit."

Reggie stared at me, tears in his eyes. He was trying so hard to understand. He slowly let out a deep sigh and said, "Yeah."

Self-Correcting Questions

Is there another way of saying it?

If that continues, will it get you
a benefit or burden?

How is that helping you?

Are you willing?

LIBK

Do you choose?

How does that help the group?

Check it out with the wisepart
within you.

LIBK
Let It Be Known

AREA: Communication, self-esteem, use of will.

COMMENT: This is a simple technique that the children enjoy. It is another way of helping them become aware of alternatives and choice of behavior.

MEDIA: Class discussion. Chalk board, chalk, eraser.

PROCEDURE: Several days before presenting the lesson, place cards with the letters LIBK around the room, on the bulletin board, on the door, on the teacher's desk. Children become very curious. When introducing it simply say, "LIBK means **Let It Be Known**." Write it on the board. Share with the children that we all have a right to let our needs and desires be known. This does not mean that we'll always get what we want. It may not be possible at the moment, it may not be best for us. However, we can **Let It Be Known**, or LIBK. When it is let known to other people in an appropriate or acceptable way, there is an excellent chance that it will work out for us.

One day Sheila hauled off and slugged Lisa sitting in the desk behind her. Lisa began yelling and crying. A game of uproar had begun. I asked Sheila why she hit Lisa. She responded:

"She kept pushing her desk against mine."

"That must have been annoying. Is there another way in which you could have let it be known?"

"Told you."

"Yes. Another way than telling the teacher?"

"Could've asked her, but she probably wouldn't stop!"

"Did you try?"

Shoulder shrug.

"Any other way?"

"Moved my desk."

"Yes, that is another possibility. Hitting other people usually brings burdens. Think of other ways of LIBKing that will be acceptable to both you and the other person."

Talking with Lisa uncovered the problem of not being able to see the board, leading to the desk-pushing episode. Looking at alternatives of Letting It Be Known so that both she and her neighbor could be winners helped bring about reconciliation.

OBSERVATION: We had been working on alternative ways of LIBK other than the usual yelling, name calling, hitting and pushing. We'd had class meetings, role playing, written assignments on the subject. I continually evoked their awareness of choice by asking, "Is there another way of letting it be known?", "Is there another way of saying it?" One morning while on yard duty I had resorted to using the old authoritarian method of yelling at some boys who were still playing after the bell rang. Kim, with some other girls, came laughing up to me, wagged a finger, and said, "Ah, ah, Mrs. Fugitt! Is there another way you can LIBK?" The delightful healing quality of humor brought an immediate change of attitude. We all laughed and shared a moment of closeness as we walked together. The children and I were both learning to self-correct and LIBK in more acceptable ways.

Feelings — Self-Esteem

THINGS I LIKE ABOUT ME

AREA: Self-evaluation and building self-esteem

COMMENT: This exercise helps to bring into the child's awareness some of the positive qualities of the personality, giving opportunity to feel good about the self and enhance self-esteem.

MEDIA: Paper and pencils, small group discussion.

PROCEDURE: Generate a discussion on things that you like in people, especially yourself. The adult may begin by naming some things she likes in herself, explaining that it is okay to like yourself and that when you feel good about yourself it is usually easier to feel good about others.

Have the children make a list of all the things they like about themselves, suggesting that if they like they may draw a picture of some of the things they list. When they have finished have them gather in groups of two or three and share the things they most like about themselves.

OBSERVATION: This is usually a happy exercise and the children get very excited about it. Sometimes they have difficulty in the beginning about thinking of positive qualities because they are not used to thinking positively about themselves.

This can be of help in assessing the child's awareness of the total self, of how much synthesis there is. If the child mentions only physical qualities, the parent or teacher will want to give more opportunities for emotional awareness or mental awareness. It can be given several times throughout the year to assess process of growth.

Things I like about me.

I like me becaue 'it cooperation with my brain.

I like me becaue I'm friendly.

I like me becaue my teacher said I improved in my work.

I like me becaue my mother said she liked me.

I like me becaue my maind can work

I like me becaue I'm 'very' bain on my math paper

I like me becaue I fill good.

I like me becaue my body is beutyful.

I like me and the world becaue it is beutyful.

I like me becaue I'm fair.

I like me becaue I'm always happy.

I like me becaue I'm good to me maind.

"I CAN. . ."

AREA: Self-awareness, self-acceptance, self-esteem.

COMMENT: This gives the child an opportunity to assess some positive elements of the personality and begin developing an awareness of strengths that lead to self-acceptance.

MEDIA: Work individually, then in twos, threes or small groups if desired. Paper and pencil.

PROCEDURE: Say to the children: "Make a list of things that you can do. Perhaps there are things that you feel very good about being able to do. List one thing that you like about yourself and one thing you think other people like about you. When you are finished find a partner and share your list."

OBSERVATION: Children with a positive self-image are able to quickly list things they can do and things they like about themselves. This is an easy tool with which to do a quick assessment of self-esteem.

Many children found this exercise to be quite difficult at first. However, as they began to accept that it was "really okay" not only to appreciate themselves but to share this appreciation, they responded with openness and joy. A sense of trust began to gradually evolve, leading to a positive awareness and acceptance of self and others.

I CAN

1. I can _____

2. I can _____

3. I can _____

4. I can _____

5. I can _____

APPRECIATE MYSELF

One thing I like about myself is _____

_____

One thing others like about me is _____

_____

IALAC AND KILLER STATEMENTS

AREA: Self awareness and acceptance, feelings, self-esteem.

COMMENT: This exercise is designed to provide the student with the awareness of negative and positive statements and alternative ways of responding to others. It provides the attitudinal words, IALAC and Killer Statements that become a tool for self awareness and self-correction.

MEDIA: Story telling, chalk board, group discussion, role playing.

PROCEDURE: The teacher makes three signs, each sign progressively smaller than the one preceding (8½ x 11 is a comfortable size for the first sign). On each sign print the letters IALAC in large capitals. The paper used should be able to tear easily.

As the story begins hold the largest sheet of paper up under the chin.

IALAC[1]

Once upon a time there was a little girl named Karen. She had a large sign across her chest with the letters, IALAC. All of us have this sign too. You have one and I have one, we just don't always see it, but it's there. Every night when Karen would go to bed she would look at her sign, give a big sigh, tuck it under her chin and go to sleep.

The next morning when she woke up she went to the bathroom and found the door locked. Her brother yelled at her, "Go away, stupid! It's my turn and I can stay as long as I want!" (Tear strip off sign, letting strip fall to floor.) Karen sighed and went back to her room. As she struggled to make her bed she asked her big sister to help her. Her sister answered, "Why should I help you, baby! I have enough to do!" (tear strip off sign).

Karen went downstairs to breakfast. Her mother yelled at her, "Hurry up! You're going to be late! What's the matter with you! Pour the orange juice and don't spill it!" (tear strip off sign). As Karen went to school she saw some friends at the corner and called to them to wait. They just laughed and ran on without waiting (tear strip off sign). As she hurried to catch up with them some boys came running behind her and pushed her down (tear strip off sign).

When Karen got to class everyone was yelling and the teacher got mad at them, saying, "All right, boys and girls, if this is the way you are going to behave we'll just have that history test now instead of next Thursday!" (tear strip off sign).

(Continue in the same vein, going through the entire day at school, the play period after school and the evening at home up to bedtime. Make every contact a negative one and tear a strip off the paper sign each time a negative statement is made.)

That night when Karen got in bed she looked at her sign, (hold up the smaller sign) saw it was much smaller, tucked it under her chin, sighed deeply and went to sleep. The next morning Karen woke up and the day continued very much like the day before, with people yelling at her (tear sign), no one having time to listen (tear sign), everyone too busy to help (tear sign) no one seeming to love her (tear sign). That night her sign was very small. She looked at it, sighed deeply, tucked it under her chin and went to sleep.

Well, what can we do to make her sign larger? Let's see what will happen to it if Karen had a day like this:

When Karen woke the next morning and went to the bathroom her brother was just finishing and said, "Hi, Karen, it's all yours!" (pick up piece of torn paper and hold under chin). As she was making her bed her big sister said, "Here, let me help you. Beds are kind of hard to make all by yourself" (pick up piece of torn paper, adding to previous piece). As Karen went to breakfast her mother said, giving her a hug, "Good morning, honey. Pour the juice and breakfast will be ready." As she walked to school her friends saw her and called that they would wait for her (pick up strip of torn paper).

When Karen got to class the teacher said, "You know, boys and girls, I've been thinking about that test I gave you and have decided that I wasn't very fair. How would it be if I just threw the test away and we talked about some of the things you need help with?" (pick up piece of paper).

(Continue the story, going through the same events of the day as told before, except this time change each negative statement to a positive statement, right up to bedtime.)

As Karen went to bed that night she looked at her sign which was larger and read, I AM LOVEABLE AND CAPABLE. She sighed happily, tucked it under her chin and went to sleep.

OBSERVATION: When this story was being told to a class of fourth graders one little boy jumped up and down and yelled, "Whoooooeeeee!" every time a "killer statement" was made and the paper was torn. He related completely to each killer statement. During the discussion following the story he said, "Every time someone said something mean to her it made her heart tear a little."

I asked the class to give some IALAC statements to list on the board. They had great difficulty in thinking of IALAC statements. They were then asked if they could list Killer statements. Killer statements are those that hurt us, cut us down, make us feel not okay. The children proceeded to fill two entire boards with Killer statements. They knew them well. After they had released all the Killer statements they seemed to be free then to list IALAC statements. I encouraged their thinking by asking, "How would you like to have it said?", showing a possible alternative.

The class then chose some of the situations listed and role played them. As the year progressed they became more comfortable with them and were able to stop and change easily.

They were encouraged to say, "Hey, you just tore my sign when you said that." I encouraged the recognition of the statements by asking, "Is there another way you can say it?" IALAC signs were made and worn for several days as reminders that they are indeed Loveable and Capable.

Good things people say
to me

Hit a home run C_____.

Let me help you do your work.

He is a verey hansum yung child.

You can loock at tv all day.

You can go and play.

Yes you can take my place.

Bad Things people say
to me

Do your own work
You cant go out side
You can not play with us.
His a verey bad child.
You can not play with yor bog

WARM FUZZIES AND COLD PRICKLIES

AREA: Self-esteem, feelings, self-correction.

COMMENT: This exercise helps to expand the child's awareness of positive and negative feelings and of the consequences of such feelings. Alternative ways of expressing and responding to these feelings are explored.

MEDIA: Listening to a story, group discussion, pencil, paper, art materials.

PROCEDURE: Children sit in a circle to listen to *The Original Warm Fuzzy Tale* by Claude Steiner, (Jalmar Press, 1977) told by the teacher. Following the story have a general discussion of receiving and giving Warm Fuzzies or Cold Pricklies. This exercise may be separated into several sessions, one for the introduction and telling of the story, another for Warm Fuzzies and another for Cold Pricklies.

Follow up activities may include role playing, listing experiences of Warm Fuzzies and Cold Pricklies, drawing pictures, writing Warm Fuzzy notes to one another, and any number of activities, depending on the creativity of the parent or teacher and children.

OBSERVATION: The children delight in this story. At the first sharing, it seems too abstract and many concrete examples must be given during the discussion period. The first time I used the story it failed miserably. One little boy thought the Warm Fuzzy was real when I likened it to a warm puppy. He immediately said with wide eyes and fearful voice, "I ain't gonna give my dog away, nobody better make me, nooooeee!" This reaction was contagious and the class immediately began rejecting the idea of Warm Fuzzies. The teacher had to wait a few weeks before presenting it again. This time she emphasized warm smiles, hugs, praise, thank yous, etc., as Warm Fuzzies, things that make you feel good. The children understood and were delighted in giving and receiving Warm Fuzzies.

They had no problem identifying Cold Pricklies. They immediately were able to make long lists of Cold Pricklies. One very helpful activity was to have the children share the experience of a Cold Prickly and then tell how they would have liked it to have been given. Could they change the Cold Prickly into a Warm Fuzzy? This was difficult at first but as the "awareness of alternatives" took place they soon were able to change.

The question, "Is that a Cold Prickly or a Warm Fuzzy?" is an excellent tool for self-correction. Or try, "If that continues (behavior or attitude) will you get a Warm Fuzzy or a Cold Prickly?" In my experience the child would pause a moment, think and correct. Nothing else would need to be said.

EXAMPLES: One afternoon the class had just finished an exciting session on Warm Fuzzies. They were grouped in twos, each pair ready to exchange a Warm Fuzzy. At first they were a little embarrassed, but as they began doing it they began glowing with smiles, wiggling like little puppies, radiating joy as they discovered good feelings about themselves and others. The room was radiant with Warm Fuzzy feelings.

At that moment a mother came angrily into the room, completely absorbed in her own needs. She yelled at her daughter to "get your things and come on!" There was a moment of stunned silence and then I said, "We are just finishing a lesson and class will be over in about five minutes. Could you please wait?" The mother then went into a tirade of anger, blasting the entire school system, yelling, swearing, and venting hostility. The class continued sitting in stunned silence and the daughter cowered in her fear, not knowing what to do.

Inwardly taking a deep breath, I smiled at the girl and quietly told her she could leave. As the two retreated down the hall, the mother could still be heard yelling and complaining about life. I turned to the class and thought, "Well, here's a perfect example; how do I use it without putting the mother down?" I said to the class, "What just happened? What did she just give to the class?" The children answered in one voice, "A COLD PRICKLY!"

"Yes, and what would help her to feel better?" The children again answered with one voice, "A WARM FUZZY!" I laughed and agreed, reminding them that "we have lots of Warm Fuzzies to share." Earlier in the year, a scene like that would have totally destroyed the class.

ATTITUDINAL VOCABULARY

AREA: Self-discipline leading to self-esteem.

COMMENT: As the exercises are used throughout the year, a common vocabulary will develop that is primarily related to choices of attitudes. As the vocabulary is referred to time and time again, the students will begin internalizing the concepts. They will be able to correct their behavior by choice, accepting with awareness the responsibility for their choice. The adult's part in disciplining will become less and less with the use of such questions as: "Will that bring a benefit or a burden?" "How does that help you?" "Is there another way you can let your need be known?" "Is that an IALAC or a Killer statement?" "Let's see if we can find some Warm Fuzzies."

Evoke and include the child's native vocabulary. Each pair of words below is a result of specific lessons taught primarily to evoke conscious awareness within the child that there are alternatives and he/she does have a choice of response.

Benefit	Burden
IALAC	Killer Statement
Warm Fuzzy	Cold Prickly
Prinze	Frozz
I'm OK	I'm not OK
Swan	Ugly Duckling

GETTING TO KNOW ME
Self-Assessment Questionnaire

AREA: Assessment of self-awareness, choice, use of will.

COMMENT: This questionnaire can be of great help in assessing where the child is in his awareness of self, of feelings, choice, and use of inner-discipline, as well as many other areas. It easily leads into follow-up activities such as discussions of concepts presented in answers, e.g., "What does 'get in trouble' mean? " visualization, journal writing, goal setting.

MEDIA: Questionnaire, pencil. Work independently first, then group discussion.

PROCEDURE: Introduce the questionnaire with comments that will help children to feel comfortable about answering it. Remind them that it is not a test, no correcting or grades will be given or recorded. They are the only ones who know the answers as the answers are about themselves and the way they feel about things. Only they know the right answer as to how they feel. This reminder is extremely important in order to release a freedom within them to answer comfortably and honestly.

OBSERVATION: When this questionnaire was given to a group of fourth graders it was first thought that it might be too long and discouraging, so the plan was to give it over a period of three days. When the children were assured that there would be no correcting or grading and the answers were about themselves, they were fantastically eager! Asked if they first wanted to discuss the questions before writing their answers they said in loud unison, "No!" and were already beginning to write. It was about a subject they knew! They finished the entire questionnaire in about twenty minutes. Most of them wrote thoughtfully and searchingly. Even the slower students were eager to answer the questions verbally if not in writing. The discussion was a joyful free-for-all of sharing and discovering about each other.

GETTING TO KNOW ME

1. Do you like yourself? _I like myself_

2. When do you like yourself? _I like myself when I am happy_

3. Do you sometimes dislike yourself? _no_

4. When do you dislike yourself? _when I am mean_
   Why? _becaus sometimes I get in trouble_

5. Do you think you are good or naughty? _In between_
   Why? _becaus sometimes get in trouble and sometimes I don't_

6. How do you tell good from bad?

   Good is _nice thing_

   Bad is _not a good poositon to be in_

7. Are you often happy or sad? _I am often happy_

8. What things make you happy? _When I get new clothes_

9. Can you choose to be happy? _yes_

10. How can you choose? _by being good_

11. What things make you most unhappy? _When I get in lots and lots of trouble._

12. Can you stop yourself from being unhappy? _sometimes I can and sometimes I can't_

13. How do you do it? *by holding my temper, going away, not listening*

14. Can you choose your feelings? *yes*   If so, how?
When I'm good to somebody

15. If you are running in the hall and a teacher tells you

    to stop, what do <u>you</u> do?

    _____   1. Keep running

    _____   2. Get mad at the teacher

    _____   3. Feel the teacher is picking on you

    __X__   4. Stop and begin walking

    __X__   5. Feel embarrassed but still OK

16. Who made you run? *myself*

17. Do you have a choice? *yes*

18. How do you feel when you have finished doing a hard math

    problem or read a hard book? *I get tired*

19. Can you work for 5 minutes without looking up from your work?
    sometimes I can.

20. When your neighbor keeps talking to you in class what can

    you do if you want to do your work?

    __X__   1. Talk with him or her.

    _____   2. Hit or kick him or her.

    __X__   3. Tell him or her to be quiet.

    _____   4. Ignore him or her.

    _____   5. Tell him or her you will talk with him at recess.

21. Whose choice is it? _mine_ Who is in charge? _me_

22. If you get mad at someone and plan to fight him or her after
    school, what happens? _I lose my temper_

23. How does this make you feel? _unhappy because_
    I wouldn't want nobody picking on
    _me._

24. Can you choose what to do? _yes_

25. What do you think the other person feels? (The one you
    are planning to fight?) _scared frightened_

26. If you get mad at your friend what do you do? _I make_
    a ugly face.

27. Is there something else you can do? _yes_

28. What? _Walk away from them._

29. Can you choose how you will feel when others call you names?
    yes

31. Do you feel people like you? _yes_
    a. If yes, why? _because I am nice to them_
    b. If no, why? _____
    c. Is there anything you can do about it? _yes_

32. Have you learned anything about yourself from answering
    these questions? _yes I can control my_
    actions

Feeling Words

When I feel bad	When I feel good
mad	confidence
lazey	understand
crazy	count on
grozy	happy
unhappy	considerate
grompy	love
uncoftable	woundeful
tereble	glad
sad	winner
mevable	countebal
loser	sorry
embarrased	forgiveing
noconfidence	silly
nounderstand	
nobody to coaraton	
sorry	

FEELING WORDS

AREA: Self-awareness, building self-esteem, basic acceptance

COMMENT: This is a basic introduction to awareness of feelings and is necessary to all the following exercises.

Identifying and claiming ownership of feelings is basic to the holistic approach to human growth. Activities involving awareness of feelings are intended to add to the developmental process of self-correction by guiding children in the basic awareness that they have feelings, that these feelings are a natural part of themselves and they have a choice as to how they will respond to these feelings.

MEDIA: General discussion, chalk board and chalk or large sheet of newsprint, drawing paper, crayons.

PROCEDURE: Generate a discussion on feelings by asking such questions as, "How do you feel when someone gives you a present?" Write the feeling word given in the answer on the board (e.g., happy). "How do you feel when you don't know your math?" Write the feeling word on the board. Continue eliciting feeling words from the group, listing as you go. Be sure to distinguish between *feeling* and *thinking* words, reminding them that feeling words are emotions and thinking words are mental. For example: the question, "How do you feel when someone cheats?" answered with, "I think it is wrong." is a feeling question with a thinking answer. An answer such as, "I feel angry." is a feeling answer, demonstrating awareness of the feeling taking place and giving it recognition.

Give the children drawing paper and have them either choose a feeling word from the list or choose how they are feeling at that moment and draw a picture of that feeling, writing the feeling word on the paper.

OBSERVATION: At first it is sometimes difficult for them to get in touch with actual feeling and feeling words. With help and lots of examples they soon become aware of the difference and are eager to share. Getting in touch with their feelings gives them an opportunity to handle them and release them. One fourth-grade girl was an extremely messy child. Every paper, her desk, everything was continually being scribbled on, smudged, torn, etc. She chose the word, "Messy." She proceeded to scribble vigorously on the paper, using very dark colors. It was truly a "messy" paper. When she finished she wadded it up, threw it away and asked for another paper. She then drew a delightful, happy picture of bright spring flowers and birds. She wrote the word "happy" on it. Permission to draw the messy feeling released within her the freedom to experience a different quality of feeling.

One little boy wrote the word "lonely" and drew a picture of a boy standing on the Golden Gate Bridge with the word "suicide" written under the bridge. He was pleading for help and this exercise enabled me to initiate that help.

See also Brian's response to a guided imagery on feelings at the end of exercise *I Feel Good When. . . I Feel Bad When. . .*

41

CAUTION: Questions such as, "What do we do with these feelings?", "Can we choose how we'll respond?", "What happens if. . .?", "Then what?" are excellent questions to evoke clarification of values. However, it is extremely important that the parent or teacher suspend judgement, imposition of his/her personal value system. Create a comfortable atmosphere that stimulates sharing freely. Call forth the child's own answers and guide him/her to assess what the appropriate response is.

EVOCATIVE WORDS

AREA: Self-actualization. Use of a word-concept to modify behavior or attitudes. Transpersonal qualities.

COMMENT: This exercise is based on the principle that energy follows thought. Every idea or image tends to produce the state of mind, the physical state, and the acts that correspond to it. Attention and repetition reinforce the effectiveness of the idea or image, be it negative or positive. The evocative word exercise evokes qualities desirable in healthy self-esteem and self-discipline.

MEDIA: Use total class discussion, large card (8½ x 11 is effective) with word-concept in large print, for the first session. Bulletin board, pencil and paper, crayon and construction paper for later sessions.

PROCEDURE: The first step for using a word-concept to modify behavior or attitudes is to choose a word that expresses the desired quality to be developed. Print the word, such as cooperation, joy, friend, will, love, freedom, etc., on the card. Have the children sit in a circle. Explain, "We are going to explore the meaning of a word and see what can be discovered about it, what it means to us." Holding the card in front of you, say the word, and say one word that describes the word for you, for example, "Cooperation-sharing." Pass the card to the next person. That person in turn says the word on the card and gives a new descriptive word for it. The card continues around the circle. Each time a new meaning is added to the chosen word. If the child can not think of a meaning he may simply say, "Pass" and hand the card to his neighbor.

Following the giving of word meanings for the evocative word, there can be a general discussion and sharing of examples and experiences with the use of the word. The parent, teacher or children may make a bulletin display or poster with the evoked word-quality (see illustration).

OBSERVATION: The class chose many evocative words. They thoroughly enjoyed the process. It was an excellent exercise in concentration as well as evoking positive qualities. The word was used in all possible ways for a given amount of time. It could be the word-quality of the month, or week. Constant reinforcement of it is important.

Evocative word: *Cooperation.*
Questions and statements such as "Let's remember the quality of cooperation as the papers are passed in," or "How is that helping to cooperate?" Place the word on small cards around the classroom as visual reminders. Encourage the use of the word in written assignments.

Evocative word: *Beauty.*
The children's life seemed so bereft of beauty that I decided to use it as the evocative word-of-the-week. By their response it quickly became apparent that their awareness and experience of beauty was indeed limited. It was most difficult for them to recall anything of beauty in their lives. We spent a week of consciously observing beauty in our environment such as the blue sky, a flower, a seagull in flight, a sunset, a cat sleeping in the sun.

A homework assignment given was: Be aware of one thing of beauty at home or on the way to and from school and how you felt when seeing it. Write one paragraph about the experience. In the beginning it was hard for the children to respond. However, as the week progressed, they became increasingly excited about their observations.

The discussions on beauty led quite naturally into discussions of feelings experienced, attitudinal and energy changes. The availability of another tool to use in the process of choosing thought forms became a part of their consciousness.

Some follow-up activities could be: drawing a symbol of beauty evoked from a visualization exercise or journal writing recalling personal experiences.

The following list includes some of the evocative words elicited from the children:

cooperation	freedom	love
courage	goodness	peace
creativity	harmony	power
beauty	joy	serenity
		truth

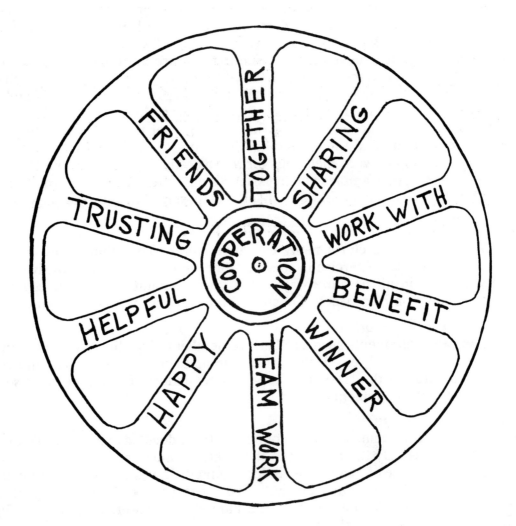

M.S.

Cooperation to share. Cooperation to be thankful. Cooperation to wait your turn. Cooperation to listen. Cooperation to raise your hand. Cooperation to do your work. Cooperation to be happy. Cooperat. to work with your mind.

pretty

3

Creative Imagination

BREATHING EXERCISE

AREA: Inner-discipline, use of will, physical awareness. Basic to all visualization exercises.

COMMENT: A very simple technique of breathing is introduced in this exercise that, when used, can change the emotional climate of a situation from one of tension and anxiety to one of serenity and receptivity.

Deep, slow, quiet breathing relaxes the body, lowering the metabolic rate and decreasing the heart and respiration rates. It also increases the alertness of the mind by increasing the supply of oxygen.

PROCEDURE:

Using a quiet, serene voice say: "Please sit quietly with your feet on the floor, legs uncrossed. Your hands may rest quietly on your lap or desk. Keep the back straight so that the lungs can function their very best. Hold the head straight and quietly close your eyes if you wish. . .now slowly take a deep breath, so silently that no one can hear you. Feel the breath going deeply into your chest, feel the chest expanding as the breath fills the chest cavity. Slowly and quietly let the breath go. Take another deep breath, again experience it, become aware of what is happening in your body as the ribs expand. Perhaps you can feel the breath going down into the abdomen. Release it now, quietly and slowly, at your own pace. Take one more breath, and simply enjoy the quiet feeling inside you."

OBSERVATION: This technique can be used with a group or individually. Once the children have learned the process it can be used at any time. It is especially helpful to use with a child who is very upset.

Karen was a child with great emotional instability. She would often get hysterical and scream and cry uncontrollably when she felt misunderstood or "unfaired" against. When she came to the fourth grade class she had a history of spending most of her time in the hall, clinging to the wall, while crying and wailing. Among many of the exercises and techniques I used with her was the quiet breathing exercise. When Karen would be so upset that she had absolutely no self-control I would quietly place my hand on the back of Karen's neck (the touch giving loving affirmation) and say very quietly, "Karen, I want to help you. I can help you better when I can understand you. Take a deep breath. Take another deep breath. That's good. I can understand you a little better. Now, take another good, deep breath and tell me what happened.''

The breathing would help Karen to quiet down and she would begin being in control of herself once more.

When giving the instructions to a group, it is important to stress doing it ''so quietly that no one can hear you.'' Children love to dramatically huff and puff. The use of the quiet voice and word ''quietly'' are important to the success of the exercise.

After taking a workshop, an elementary principal decided that he'd try the breathing exercise with the children. At the next school assembly he said without any introduction, ''Now boys and girls, let's all take a deep breath.'' Utter chaos ensued — huffing and puffing, turning blue in the face, etc. Do take time to give quiet guidance.

Suggested Resources:

Carr, Rachel. *Yoga For All Ages*. (New York: Simon and Schuster, Inc., 1972).

Dechanet, J. M. *Christian Yoga*. (New York: Harper and Row, Inc., 1972).

Hendricks, Gay. Wills, Russel. *The Centering Book*. (New Jersey: Prentice-Hall, Inc., 1975).

PREPARATION FOR GUIDED IMAGERY

AREA: Self-esteem and inner-discipline with use of the creative imagination. Concentration skills.

COMMENT: The alignment or process of preparation for a guided imagery exercise is extremely important in establishing the student's receptivity and determining the quality of success.

PROCEDURE: Remind the children that guided imagery uses that part of the mind that creates, imagines, dreams. "Everything that happens in the imagination is all right, so don't take time to think about it, just let it happen and experience it. If you don't like it you may 'erase' it in your imagination. Remember, you are always in charge. You are the creator. Later, after it is over, you may want to process it through that part of your mind that thinks and knows right from wrong."

With the children sitting quietly, lead them through the steps of breathing as described in the Breathing Exercise. As the body quietly relaxes, the mind remains alert and is able to concentrate. After the first few breaths, suggest that as they exhale they let all the feelings of negativity experienced that day go with the breath.

"Just let that feeling go. . .the feeling of anger, hurt, jealousy. . .whatever it is, just let it go as you let the breath go out of your body, knowing that you may deal with it later if you wish. As you inhale, breathe in the feeling of quietness, of being okay." Begin imagery.

OBSERVATION: Some children have great difficulty with this at first because of the inability to concentrate. This is an excellent exercise to develop concentration. Do not insist that the eyes be closed but suggest that it will be more fun and they will be able to "see" in their imagination better with the eyes closed. As they become comfortable with it they become more trusting and are eager to sit quietly and close the eyes.

IMAGERY
A Trip to the Woods

AREA: Self-discipline, use of the creative imagination, use of the will. Transpersonal quality of serenity.

COMMENT: Imagination is a function which in itself is to some extent synthetic, since imagination can operate at several levels concurrently; those of sensation, feeling, thinking and intuition.

This exercise uses the creative imagination to help the child experience a sense of serenity and develop an awareness that he can direct his thoughts toward achieving a particular attitude by use of the imagination.

It is excellent to use as a transition. At the end of this exercise children will move quietly and cooperatively into the next subject or task. It releases tension, evokes the quality of serenity and calmness. It rests the body, emotions and mind, releasing energy to handle life a little more creatively.

MEDIA: The children sit quietly with eyes closed, listening and visualizing the guided imagery as directed by the parent or teacher.

At first most children are reluctant to close their eyes. Gently encourage them, assuring them they'll be able to experience more if they do, but it is okay if they need to keep the eyes open. It is the degree of self-confidence and trust that permits them to close the eyes. By the end of several sessions they are comfortably closing their eyes.

PROCEDURE: Always use the Preparation For Guided Imagery process to begin visualization. Have the children sit in their seats, in a large circle, or independently in the room. The children are sitting quietly in a relaxed posture but with backs straight and head up. Explain that the brain functions better when the back is straight and the lungs can breathe better, sending oxygen to the brain. Have the children take three slow, deep breaths, so silently that no one can hear them. Slowly release the breath. This helps to quiet the body and the mind in preparaton for the imagery.

Begin in a quiet voice by explaining:

Today we are going to take a short trip. We are going to use our imagination, that part of our mind that sees pictures and can create. We're going to take a trip to the woods. As you breathe quietly, imagine that you are walking down a path in the woods. It is a friendly woods, a lovely day. The sun is shining and you feel it on your skin, warm and comfortable. A gentle breeze blows on you, feeling fresh and good. The sun sparkles on the leaves of the trees. The air smells oh, so good, a woodsy scent. The earth feels firm under your feet and you rustle the leaves with your feet as you walk. As the path curves, you come to a lovely stream. It is cool and inviting.

You sit on a rock, just the right size for you, and look at the water. It is sparkling in the sun, bubbling and singing as it tumbles along. You could easily wade the stream if you wished. But you continue to sit on the rock, with your feet comfortably dangling in the cool water. You take a deep breath and simply enjoy it. The sky is blue above you. All is silent and peaceful. You watch a leaf float gently down from a tree and glide and twirl in the stream. You hear the birds singing and rejoice. . . You feel very good deep down inside you. There is no pressure for you to do anything. Everything is just right. You can stay there as long as you wish. [Pause]

As you look around, you see a deer come out of the woods across the stream and walk to the edge of the water. It pauses and looks around. You sit very quietly, looking across at this beautiful deer. You think loving thoughts about it and silently, in your mind, you send it reassuring thoughts that everything is okay and you are its friend. It stands there, quietly returning your look and seems to know that it can trust you. It dips its head and takes a drink. Then slowly and quietly looking around, it returns into the woods.

You continue sitting there for a while, just feeling good about yourself, about the beauty of the deer, and the woods, and just good about everything. You know that you are okay.

Now, in your own time, quietly return up the path from which you came and return to the room. Be aware of your body sitting in the chair, and your feet touching the floor. Hear the sounds in the room. When you are ready, open your eyes.''

OBSERVATION: The children love this exercise. They often ask for it after coming in from a busy, frustrating, everything-gone-wrong type of lunch period. One little fourth grader came swinging into the room one day saying, ''Let's go to the woods, I need a vacation!'' Indeed, he had had a rough time at recess.

An 83-year-old volunteer grandmother said, ''I don't know what happens, but it's mystical.''

CAUTION: With children, always make guided imagery safe, such as: ''The rock is just the right size for you.'' (Choice) The animal is a gentle one (purpose is for relaxation), and on the other side of the stream (safe distance). ''It can trust you'' (self-worth, transpersonal quality of trust evoked).

Quietly bring the children back to the reality of the room by having them become aware of their physical body, sounds, room environment.

I observed a group of teachers being led in a guided imagery involving the seashore in which safety guides were not given. One woman was so obedient to the guide (who had neglected to provide points of choice), that she became hysterical because she couldn't swim. In a group situation extra precautions must be made not to evoke excessive fear, especially if the purpose of the guided imagery is for relaxation!

IMAGERY
A Trip to the Beach

AREA: Self-discipline and self-acceptance, use of the creative imagination and will.

COMMENT: This exercise uses the creative imagination to help the child get in touch with the inner part of himself that experiences serenity and calmness and in turn produces a measure of self-confidence and self-acceptance.

MEDIA: No materials needed. Children sit in a circle or at desks with eyes closed, listening and visualizing the guided imagery as directed by the adult.

PROCEDURE: Have the children sit wherever they choose or as directed. They sit quietly in a relaxed posture but with backs straight and head up. Quietly remind them that the brain functions better when its source of oxygen is good. This is helped when the lungs have plenty of room to inhale the oxygen and they do this better when the back is straight.

Begin in a quiet voice, remembering that you are painting a picture with words.

"Today we are going to take a trip to the beach. We are going to use our imagination, that part of our mind that sees pictures and can create anything we wish. In preparation for the trip quietly and slowly take three or four deep breaths. Breathe so quietly that no one can hear it. Hold the breath for a moment and slowly release it. As you do this, be aware of your body becoming quiet and still and your mind becoming quiet and alert.

Now lift your thoughts to that place of imagination and make-believe, and visualize yourself on a beautiful beach. The sun is warm and gentle. The cool sea breeze blows gently on you. The weather is just right for you. Lie down on the sand and feel the gentle warmth of the sand beneath you. You close your eyes and listen to the sound of the ocean waves breaking and rolling in a quiet rhythm. . . You hear the cry of sea gulls and watch them flying lazily in the blue sky. . . You feel good, at peace. You lie there looking at the white fluffy clouds, the sea gulls, smelling the fresh salt air, listening to the rhythm of the ocean. . .feeling the warm sand. All is good and you feel very good. There is no hurry, you don't have to do anything, no one is demanding that you do this or that. It is good. You know that you are okay. Just lie there on the sand for awhile and experience the beauty of the day. [Pause. . .]

Now, when you are ready, in your own time, sit up on the beach and quietly return to the room. (Allow time for this quiet transition.)"

OBSERVATION: This, like all nature imagery trips, brings about a complete change of emotional climate. The children always enjoy it. The more frequently these exercises are used the more they become accustomed to them and the more readily they respond. It is important to always do the preparation of quiet breathing, as this sets the stage.

As the children learn to trust their images and grow in self-confidence they will change even more. The imagery has taken the child through a positive experience of the bodily senses of touch, smell, sound and sight. The emotions have quieted to a sense of well-being, of serenity and a good sense of self-esteem. The mind has rested and experienced creativity. This five-minute exercise is so much easier to use as a transition of mood than a lecture of "shoulds" and "oughts." It releases energy and encourages student receptivity to creative work.

CAUTION: Whenever creating images of weather, water, rocks, etc., always be sure to state that it is "just the right" size or right depth or right. . .for you. This places trust in the child's inner knowing of what is best for him and eliminates possible fears of the water being too deep or the rock too high, etc. Use all the words possible to make it a comfortable experience while still permitting the child dignity of choice.

Do speak slowly, allowing time for visualization to occur. A careful balance is needed of neither rushing nor dragging the process.

IMAGERY
I Feel Good When. . . I Feel Bad When. . .

AREA: Self-awareness, inner-discipline, use of will, feelings.

COMMENT: This exercise encourages awareness of negative and positive feelings. It provides opportunity to go within the self and explore these feelings, helping to bring forth recognition of the feelings and acceptance of responsibility for the feelings experienced. The words *good, bad* are value judgements. The parent or teacher needs to be careful not to impose his/her values in this exercise. Evoke feelings from the children. Let them make their own assessments.

MEDIA: Imagery, pencil, crayons, and paper. Work individually, then in small groups.

PROCEDURE: Lead the children into a receptive attitude for an imagery trip by having them sit quietly, breathing deeply and silently. . .the body is still, the hands and feet are resting quietly. Take several deep breaths to help rest the body and give alertness to the mind. . .(see exercise on breathing). ''Now, lift your consciousness up to that part of your mind that imagines, that creates, that sees pictures. Using that part of your mind, you are now going to explore some feelings you have had.

Think of a time when you felt badly. . .perhaps sad or lonely. . .maybe hurt, felt like crying. . .or very angry. . .ashamed. . .embarrassed. . . Stay with one feeling and visualize the time you felt that way. See what was happening. What were you doing? Can you see yourself? How do you look? Now, since this is in your imagination and you are in charge, do something in that scene that will help you feel better. What can you do that will change that first feeling? Something that only you can do. . . Now that you have done this, what are you doing? What is happening? How are you feeling now? . . . Experience that good feeling. . .it may be happy, joyful, calm, tender, caring. . .friendly. . .powerful. Let it be a part of you. Appreciate it.

Continue sitting quietly for a few moments and when you are ready, write in your journal about what you experienced. Remember the time when you felt bad and what you did to change that feeling to a good feeling.

When you are finished writing, you may share with a partner if you wish.''

CAUTION: Be sure to have all materials placed in front of each student *before* beginning the process. This permits a continuous flow of creative energy without interruption. Nothing can break this flow so quickly as having a mad scramble for materials following the guided imagery.

OBSERVATION: Use after concept of feelings is well established. When children have been quietly led through a guided imagery process there is always a response of deep silence. They will quietly write or draw at great length, totally immersed within their own process. Children who would greet a routine writing assignment with great resistance would write without stopping for twenty to thirty minutes in complete silence. Their penmanship and spelling would flow effortlessly while in the creative energy stream. They owned the story.

"Anger" is Brian's response to a guided imagery on feelings. Brian was a tall, athletic boy who came to me in the fourth grade and stayed through the fifth grade. When he arrived he had a long history of a quick temper, much fighting. We did a lot of work together in those two years. His self-awareness and self-esteem expanded with the ability to respond with choice, to self-correct. He graduated from the sixth grade with honors in athletics, music and academic achievement.

Anger

Today I had a lot of anger when my sister lost the lunch money. But when she found it I was relly happy. I have the same problem at home I get agery and just fight somebody. Somtime I get mad and go some place just to get a way from someone. I gess I get a lot of angers in me that just wont quite. Some of my angers went go away they just stay there and just take controll of me and just let me go a head and fight

IMAGERY
More Nature Trips

AREA: Creative Imagination, use of the will, self-discipline and self-acceptance.

COMMENT: All imagery trips that have nature as the theme exercise the use of the creative imagination, the use of the will. They have the ability to bring forth an attitude of serenity and receptivity. A synthesis of the physical, emotional, mental and higher, creative self is experienced. They offer the child an excellent tool for transition of moods, feelings, experiences, restoring self-confidence and self-esteem through self awareness.

MEDIA: No materials needed. Children sit quietly with closed eyes, listening and visualizing the guided imagery directed by the teacher.

PROCEDURE: Use the same procedure as in the previous nature imagery trips. Remember always to begin with the alignment process of good posture, quiet breathing, calling forth the creative, imaginative part of the mind.

"Trips" to the desert, experiencing the beauty of a flower unfolding, to the top of a mountain with a panoramic view, trips into space and the stars are all possible topics. Awareness of still being part of the universe even though very small, the sense of being a part of life, of belonging, is developed. The adult uses the imagination to gently and creatively paint a word picture that will be translated into attitudes of serenity, calmness, self-assuredness, acceptance and awareness of being okay.

After the children have had several guided trips, they may wish to have a discussion on some of their responses to the trips. This can be a means for the parent or teacher to assess the effectiveness of the exercises.

VISUALIZATION

AREA: Creative imagination, inner authority, act of will, focus, choice.

COMMENT: Visualization is a powerful tool and when used wisely it becomes a most effective and versatile means of calling forth from within the child the ability to be his/her most creative self. The use of the creative imagination is based on what Assagioli states is a fundamental fact and law: "Every image has in itself a motor-drive" or "images and mental pictures tend to produce the physical conditions and the external acts corresponding to them." This is a basic principle used in psychosynthesis.

The indications and applications of visual techniques are extensive. They include all the various types of imagination, such as visualization — the evocation of visual images, auditory imagination, tactile, kinesthetic imagination, and so on.

MEDIA: Individual, small group or entire class. No materials unless needed for followup such as pencil, paper, art materials.

PROCEDURE:

1. *Visualization used for transition from one activity to another:*

This is a most effective exercise to use at the beginning of a lesson, or when children have just come in from recess and are unable to focus on the task.

Lead the children in the relaxation process as described in the Preparation For Guided Imagery. When they are relaxed and quietly receptive, say something to the following effect:

"Now, quietly go to that place in your mind where you can create and imagine. See yourself, in your imagination, working comfortably from now until the bell rings. Choose the attitude you will have. (Be sure to have had a previous discussion on definition of attitudes.) How will the attitude you choose help you?. . . What materials will you need?. . How will you get them?. . . If you need help, who will you ask?. . . (Pause between each question, allowing time for silent response.) Where will you sit?. . . See yourself, your neighbor and the entire class working comfortably together. . . Experience this comfortable feeling. . . Rest for a moment in the silence, and when you are ready, open your eyes and begin your work."

At the end of a short visualization such as this there is a hushed, relaxed quiet in the room. As the children experience relaxation, they are able to concentrate and make internal choices. They will quietly begin working, moving about the room if the work requires it, helping where needed, being creatively independent. I, too, benefit from this exercise and am able to teach with greater focus and support.

This exercise can be used for almost any activity done in the classroom. Its purpose is to facilitate the ability of the child to focus on a given task with full creative expression.

2. *Visualization before changing room environment.*

The usual process of moving desks, pushing tables, placing chairs in a circle can be noisily chaotic to say the least. A moment of quiet visualization before furniture moving can create a complete change in behavior.

Quietly lead the children in the relaxation process. (As the children become skilled in the process they are able to do it quite quickly.)

Suggest that they lift their thoughts to that creative place of imagination. "Choose the behavior you will have during the class meeting or the movie (whatever the situation may be). Visualize where you will place your chair. What do you need to do to help prepare the circle? See in your imagination where you will place your desk. See yourself quietly doing your part to help us get ready. When you are ready to do it, open your eyes and begin."

The quiet moment of visualization provides an opportunity to make a behavioral choice, to create a plan of response. The children push and shove furniture with a minimum of effort and time. No, they do not become controlled robots. They simply have a greater awareness of individual choice and responsibility to the process of the moment.

3. *Visualization before an art lesson.*

A first grade teacher came to me in complete frustration one morning after the children had been working with clay. She said, "I thought they said children were supposed to be free and creative! Ha!" These children weren't. One little girl was hysterically crying because, "Mine doesn't look like hers!" Another child kept punching and banging his clay, "I don't know what to make." The negative "I can't" thoughtforms along with the heresy of comparison soon spread their energies like wildfire. The teacher said it was chaos. She was exhausted.

We talked about the possibilities of doing a moment of relaxation and visualization before they began the clay work. A few days later the teacher came floating into the lunch room to share about, "the most fantastic morning with clay!" She had the clay on the desks before each child and led them in the following visualization:

"Close your eyes and breathe quietly. Be aware of your breathing. Breathe so silently no one can hear except you. Experience your body becoming quiet, your mind becoming alert. In that quiet space go in your imagination to that place where you can create, can make things just the way you want.

Now, in your mind's eye, see the lump of clay. Inside that clay is something very special. It is special for you. It is waiting for you to discover it. . .for you to bring it into shape. Still in your imagination, look at that special object. See its shape. Just think the answer, don't say it out loud. Is it round?. . .square?. . .oblong? Is it tall?. . .short?. . .fat? . . .thin? Is it smooth?. . .rough? What is it? Look at it. In your imagination see your fingers molding the clay, shaping the object just the way you want it to be, the way you see it now. It is yours, it belongs to you. It is waiting for you to create it. Continue looking at it for a few moments, see if you want to add something, change something. . . When you are willing, return your thoughts to the room. Open your eyes and begin working with the clay in front of you."

The children worked in almost complete silence, intent in their own creative expression. Each child "owned" the creation. He had seen it in his own place of creativity. No comparison was needed. They were able to share their experience and enjoy the creations of their neighbors.

The teacher said it was unbelievable. She was alive with energy.

4. *Visualization before creative writing.*

A few moments of quiet visualization before a written assignment can stimulate a creative flow that will produce some excellent writings. It is far more effective than the traditional, sterile instruction to, "Write about. . ."

Have the children make journals as an art project. Tell them that the journals will be for their creative writing and drawings. Emphasize that the work in the journals will not be judged or graded, will not be a part of the report card evaluation. This relieves the anxiety of "having to produce" and releases creative energy. Language skills are taught at a different time. It is interesting to note how smoothly the language skills flow without the pressure of grades and following a period of visualization in which the children contact their own unique way of expression.

Use the same visualization technique as described in the above exercises.

When the relaxation and Preparation for Guided Imagery steps are completed you may wish to guide them in the following visualization.

Say, in your own words, something such as:

"Now that we have created these lovely journals let's create a special place where we can go in our mind to create. This is a place, for imagination purposes only, that we can create to be anything we want it to be. It is a place where we feel very good about ourselves, where we can be alone or invite only the people we wish to have with us. It is a very private place.

This is a place of beauty, of quiet, of joy. Whenever you are feeling not OK, or have something hard to do and need a place to think, you can create this place in your mind for a few minutes.

Take a look at this special place you are creating. What does it look like? Where is it? Is it an inside place? Is it an outside place? How large is it? What is its shape? Do you go up or down to it? Create a place to sit and write. What will you write on? What is its size? Its shape? Is it hard? Soft? What does it feel like? What else is there? What are the colors? Remember, you are in charge. You may add or change anything you wish.

Take a moment and look around at this special place. See yourself in it. Are you comfortable? Is there anything else you need to make it a special place of beauty, quiet, joy for you?

When you are comfortable with it, become aware of the sounds here in the classroom. Be aware of your body sitting in the chair and the people in the room. When you are ready, open your eyes and begin writing in your journal."

Whenever the journals are to be used, a brief recall of the children's own special place for writing is evoked.

Sometimes following a creative writing session the children can be invited to find a partner and share. They usually do this with great eagerness and pride. It is theirs. They have "seen" it. They have created it. They can change it. They are in charge.

CAUTION: The emphasis on "for imagination purposes only" helps the child to keep imagination and reality in balance. "For a few minutes" is a safety precaution for the child who may use it for an inappropriate escape from reality. Remember to pause between questions, allowing time for the creative process to take place.

M. A.

In My Own Place

    I went to a place where nobody knows about it. It has a desk so I can write on it a chair to go with the desk. The desk and chair was white and gold. I sat there thinking of what to write. Then something went pop! in my head It was a great idea. I then began to write peoms and story and almost anything I could think of. I then stop I had a nother idea. I put the peoms and story together. I had wrote a book. I never wrote a book before.

    I felt good inside. I had wrote ten book in a mouth.

My Little Cottage

I seen a little cottage in the forest and nobody nows where it is. I swim in the pond and play with the animals. I take a big breath and let it out and started running in the forests as fast as I can until I got to the place I wanted to be at. A certian place what has flowers trees everything I enjoy its a place I go to everyday. To sing dance and even often I show some one where my little cottage is at. And then I hear a shot and another I go to see what is happying and I see that a hunter is firing at a deer but the deer gets away. And the hunter turns away and leaves my forest of bruty and joy. I wish that no one no one will find my little cottage where the pond and my flowers and trees our at.

The End

CREATIVE IMAGINATION

This delightful bit of honesty was a fifth grader's response to an exercise in visualizing the attitude she would like her teammates to have.

An imagination is a thing or person I like very much. You can do anything you want like make a bird without wings or a story like the one I just finished P.S. I love to see every body happy but sometimes I can't because for some reason or another I don't like can't stand some People

EVALUATION

I am often asked how I can be sure the child will continue using these skills. I can't be sure. I know only that some seeds of self-awareness and self-correction have been planted. Hopefully as the child's life unfolds, some of the skills will be recalled in time of need.

The sixth grade teacher gave her class an assignment to write about something that had been especially helpful to them, something that they had learned while attending elementary school. She gave me the following responses.

B. W. *

Journals

One thing that I learned in Mrs Fugitt class is how to control my self. The things she taught me was benefits and burdens. I use burdens just before I plan to hit somebody. Then I think about the burden. I might have to write or go home. Then I think about benefits if I dont hit him then I wont get into trouble. Burdens and benefits are two good words to think about. Im in the sixth grade now I was in the fifth when I had these words.

*The same child who wrote about Anger, page 60, when in the fifth grade.

Journal

When I was in Mrs. Fugitts class for 4, and 5 grade I learned alot about benefits, and burdens, and how to set my own goul. I use most of these benefits, burdens, and gouls today as I sit in my class. Like on the C.T.B.S test I used alot of imagination, and thinking back to what all I learned in Mrs. Fugitts class two years ago. I think I did a good job on the test.

In Mrs. Fugitts class we did alot of imaginating in our journals, we wrote alot of stories just by imaginating. I remember how she did it. We closed our eyes sat down straight up and relaxed our selves, and then she started talking about what we would write about for 5 minutes. Then we would write about what she was talking about. When I do assignments now I still imagine what I am going to write about.

4

Inner Authority

THE WISE PART WITHIN

AREA: Self-esteem, self-awareness, self-correction, act of will, choice, Transpersonal Self.

COMMENT: This is a technique designed to help the child get in touch with the part within him that is always in perfect harmony with life. The recognition of self as used in psychosynthesis, i.e., recognition of the "wise part" or unifying center of the self, is developed so that the child will have a tool or guide to help the process of making the best possible choice she/he is capable of making. It is through this awareness of self that self-esteem and sense of inner authority come. The basic purpose of psychosynthesis is to release or help release the energies of the Self.

MEDIA: Class Discussion

PROCEDURE: To introduce the concept of the Wise Part Within simply say something to the following effect:

   "There is a wise part within all of us. There is a wise part within you. A wise part within me. A wise part deep within everyone you know. The wise part in you is so wise that it knows what is right for you far more than I. It is so wise it evens knows what is right for me and what is right for the group.

   "One of the ways to get in touch with that wise part within is to sit quietly, take several deep breaths, so silently that you can hear the sounds in the next room. Breathe slowly, at your own rhythm. As you experience your body becoming quiet, you may wish to visualize in that creative place in your mind a lovely flower or a white fluffy cloud in a blue sky. You may visualize a diamond or a star above your head. Experience the silence. In that silence you may ask the wise part within for the help you need."

OBSERVATION: Assagioli calls it the Transpersonal Self. Jung calls it the Higher Self. James calls it the Deep Center. In an attempt to simplify a highly complex concept, to put it in the language of children, I call it the Wise Part Within. The children seem to intuitively know what is meant by these words and respond dramatically to them. I have often been asked by teachers, "What do parents say?" My response has been that I've never had a parent deny that his/her child has a wise part within him. I shared this concept and how I use it with the parents of my children. I led them in an exercise of getting in touch with the wise part deep within themselves. They responded, as did the children, with instant, intuitive recognition and acceptance of the concept, giving full support to teaching it to their children.

JUAN

A high school science teacher learned this concept and technique in one of my workshops. She reported almost with awe the results of using it with a student "whose main purpose in life seemed to be to see how much disturbance he could create in the classroom." She, a tiny woman, said this huge high school senior was towering over her, being his usual disturbing self, when she inwardly gulped and decided to try it. She said, "You know, Juan, there is a very wise part deep within you. That wise part knows what is right for you. It knows better than I or anyone else what is right for you. Will you take a quiet breath and contact that wise part? You don't have to give me an answer." (Honor the student's privacy. The resulting behavior will give you the answer.) He stopped, stared at her, stood silently for a moment, turned and walked to a seat in the back of the room. He slumped down, remaining in silence for the rest of the period. She reported that was great progress for him. Something had been touched, been identified, been honored with the dignity of choice.

ANGELA

One morning I heard myself angrily using my most authoritarian voice with Angela, a fifth grader. Angela had returned from a week's absence due to illness. When a child is out for a period of time it always takes a while to re-establish the "pecking order." She had been quite restless, disturbing her teammates and the rest of the class. There was a lot of restless energy in the class that morning, including mine. I told Angela, using the strong, no-nonsense voice teachers and parents are so capable of using, to step out in the hall until I could speak with her. Angela, an attractive little girl from Guatemala, stomped out of the room, muttering and posturing — "Sooo!" In the hall I launched into the usual authoritarian pitch of how this behavior can't continue, etc. I heard myself saying, "If this continues, Angela, I'll have to call your father." I also heard Angela angrily yelling back, "So, call my father!"

We were both caught in the tit-for-tat game of survival of the egos or making each other losers. As we stood with arms crossed on chest, glaring and making demands on each other, I heard another part of me thinking, "What am I doing? I don't want to call her father! I don't want to take her to the office! I don't want to fill out triplicate forms!" As these thoughts entered my consciousness, I was able to say, "Oh, Angela, I don't like hearing what we are saying to each other. Maybe we had better take a deep breath and get in touch with the wise part within us." She stopped and stared at me. I quietly took a deep breath and briefly closed my eyes. Angela did the same. As we silently looked at each other, I smiled and she burst into tears, threw her arms around me and cried, "Oh, Mrs. Fugitt!" My arms went around her and we experienced the healing of reconciliation.

A common understanding of a basic concept in right relations, a common vocabulary, a point of choice, an act of will, a bonding of student-teacher relationship, or an opportunity to stop, self-correct in the middle of the process is much more effective than those triplicate forms!

BRETT

Brett angrily knocked papers and books off his desk and stomped out of the room. I followed him. I asked him where he was going. Chin thrust in air, arms folded on chest, he defiantly replied, "Call my mother! She said I don't have to do nothin' you said!" Brett's mother was full of hostility and vented it quite regularly on the teachers and school system in general.

This was a day on which I happened to be centered. I took a few quiet, deep breaths (a highly effective tool in times of behavioral crises) and thought, "How do I help him? What can I say that will reach him?" As I quietly looked at him, the image of Brett a few days ago with his Bible came to mind. He had brought his Bible to school and eagerly shared that he was learning "memory verses" and would get an award at Sunday School. I do not encourage teachers to "preach" or "moralize" to children. However, at that moment, responding to the image, I purposefully chose to speak in a language he could understand. I asked Brett if he remembered when he brought his Bible to school a few days ago. He stared angrily at me. I asked him what the memory verses taught him about how to behave and if they had anything to do with "good behavior" at school.

Brett stared at me. His rich brown skin turned ashen. An awareness, a connection was taking place deep within him — a connection of Sunday School teachings with his school behavior. It was so strong that he simply stared, turned, walked back to the room, picked up the spilled materials and began working — all in silence.

When awareness is present, correction can take place.

TACELIA

We had been discussing feelings and how hard it was sometimes to do things, especially when it was something new. The children were familiar with the term Higher Self. Tacelia said, "Well, all you have to do is get in touch with your Upper Self and then do it!"

Dr. Albert Schweitzer states, "We are at our best when we give the doctor who resides within each patient a chance to go to work."[1] To paraphrase this for parents and teachers I would say we are at our best when we give the teacher who resides within each child a chance to go to work.

1. Quoted in Norman Cousins, *Anatomy of An Illness*; (New York: W. W. Norton and Co., 1979), p. 69.

DIS-IDENTIFICATION

AREA: Self-realization, self-esteem, act of will, discrimination, self-correction. To be used *after* Feeling exercises are taught.

COMMENT: This exercise enhances a sense of self-hood, a sense of being, a sense of identity, the sense of a center within oneself.

Dis-identification is a process through which children learn the lessons of objectivity and self-discrimination. Children, as well as adults, are often subject to the pull of their physical, emotional and mental demands, having no sense of choice, direction or power. When they can dis-identify from the problem, pull away from the demands, the energies can then be directed at will, evoking higher energies that can be applied creatively to life.

MEDIA: Class discussion, chalk board, chalk and eraser.

PROCEDURE: Begin in a simple conversational tone by saying something to the following effect:

"Today we are going to talk about ourselves, about who we are. Remember when you were in the second and third grade and you learned about sets, subsets and universal sets in math?" (Briefly review mathematical concept, drawing on board. The numbers $6 + 2$ are subsets of set 8. The numbers $7 + 1$ are subsets of 8, etc. The number 8 is also a part of the universal set of all numbers.)

"Each of us also has many subsets. Each of us is an individual set with many subsets. Each of us is also a part of a universal set. We have many parts.

"Each of us has a body. But we are more than our body, more than just our arms, legs, etc. (elicit some names of body parts from children). We use our body to serve us in many ways (elicit from children). We have a body, but are not our body. We are more.

Each of us has emotions — feelings, many feelings, such as anger, jealousy, sadness, happiness, joy (elicit list from children). However, we are not our feelings. We use the feelings to help express ourselves. For instance, I have anger but I am not anger. I am more than anger. I have joy, but I am not joy. I am more than joy. We are more than a body or a feeling.

Each of us has an intellect — intelligence, but we are not our intelligence. We use our intelligence just as we use our body and feelings, to express our individuality in its own unique, creative way. We are a self that is over and above each of these parts. We are a self that is greater than just a body, emotions, and intellect. For instance, I am a center of pure consciousness. I am a self that is capable of directing and using all parts of me, my body, my emotions and my mental abilities. That which calls itself "I" is a part of all of life, just as the number 8 is a part of all numbers. (Explore further with discussion, questions, responses.)

OBSERVATION: We dis-identify, or separate from the part to be able to gain perspective and right proportion. As this is achieved, we can begin taking charge of our lives. We learn to control our bodies, feelings and thoughts rather than letting them control us. The ability to focus, to have purposeful and creative lives, is developed. A positive self-esteem is established as well as the ability to self-correct. The process of synthesizing the different aspects from which we have dis-identified becomes possible, bringing the parts into unity and a harmonious whole.

Example of children applying the concept of dis-identification to their own behavior are given in the section on subpersonalities.

My Subpersonalities

I have a part in me that is called Miss Chatter Box. She likes to talk a lot.

I got another part that wants to learn very much about other thing in the world and she is call Miss Learn It all.

I have a part in me that likes to eat a lot when she comes home and she is Fat Dumpling.

I have a part in me that is called Miss Laughing Hyena.

I have a part in me that likes to play and have the time of her life and she is called The Player.

I have a part in me that reads reads and reads that she stays in one place and reads. She is called The Non Stopable Reader.

I have a part in me who likes to play instruments. She is called Miss Mucic Girl.

SUBPERSONALITIES

AREA: Dis-identification, self-correction, act of will, inner authority, self-esteem.

COMMENT: This technique is to be taught in conjunction with the lesson on dis-identification. It enhances the child's ability to be an observer of his/her behavior, to gain a sense of objectivity. The objectivity, or dis-association from the situation or emotional response, permits the child to discover an alternative course of action. The freedom of choice becomes a conscious act.

The study, understanding, and discovery of subpersonalities is an involved process. It is a major part of the psychosynthesis work. Ferrucci describes subpersonalities as "psychological satellites, coexisting as a multitude of lives within the overall medium of our personality." For a greater understanding of subpersonalities Piero Ferrucci's book, *What You May Be* is recommended.

MEDIA: Class discussion, small groups. Paper, journals, pencils, drawing paper, crayons.

PROCEDURE: If possible, have the children sit in a circle. This provides an atmosphere of informality and a sense of group sharing. Introduce the subject of subpersonalities by saying in some way similar to the following:

"Have you ever noticed that you behave differently in school than at home? Differently on the playground than in the classroom? Or differently when you're at a party from the way you behave in church? How you behave as a son/daughter or a brother/sister?"

Have children respond, sharing the various ways in which they behave. They may respond in dyads or in the whole group. Encourage them by sharing an example in your own life, e.g., how you behave in the classroom and how you behave at home.

"All of us behave differently in different situations. One way of identifying these parts is to call them subpersonalities. (Take time to define 'sub' as being a part of the whole. Evoke ideas from children.) For instance, I have a part in me, that we'll call a subpersonality, who likes to clown around. At a party it is perfectly appropriate to clown around, to act silly and have fun. However, if I let that clown subpersonality play at an important meeting or when I'm sitting in church, then it is inappropriate. Since I'm in charge of my subpersonality, I can simply tell it to stop. I can tell it that it may play at another time."

Evoke from the children a list of subpersonalities, writing them on the chalk board as given. Suggest that they may give them names. A follow-up may be to have them list their own subpersonalities and share with a partner if they wish.

OBSERVATION: The concept of subpersonalities has been simplified for the children. The primary intent is to provide another tool with which to gain greater self-control and sense of inner-authority. The methods and exercises to expand this concept are as unlimited as the adult's creativity. Journal writing, visualization exercises, identifying various subpersonalities, symbols, art-drawing of subpersonalities are but a few of the possibilities.

My Subpersonalities

1. I have a chatter-box.
2. I have a running rudy.
3. I have a frown fanny.
4. I have a happy heather.
5. I have a lazy lucy.
6. I have a jealous jenny.
7. I have a mean mandy
8. I have a silly sue.
9. I have a walker wilma.
10. I have a abby artist.
11. I have a noisy nancy.
12. I have a thinking thelma
13. I have a dancing dorris.
14. I have a writting wanda.
15. I have a smart susie.
16. I have a cookie monster.
17. I have a reading ruth.
18. I have a homework hater.
19. I have a creative Candy.
20. I have a playing Pat.

THE TIMER

"I'm not going to do it!" All the books and papers went crashing to the floor with one angry push from Lamont. The class had just been given a language assignment.

I silently took a deep breath and looked at Lamont, thought for a moment and said, "Wow! Sounds like that subpersonality with the temper is really angry. How long, Lamont, do you think it needs to be angry? Remember, you're in charge of it. Check it out. Does it need five minutes? Ten minutes? All day? Ten years?"

Lamont glared at me.

"Tell you what, Lamont. There's a timer on my desk. Decide how long you're going to let that subpersonality be in charge of you, get the timer and set it for the amount of time you're willing to give it."

Lamont glared, stomped to the desk and grabbed the timer. He angrily stomped back to his seat and set the timer. Slamming the timer down, he then turned his back to the class with much posturing and stared out the window.

I smiled and didn't say anything. The class had silently observed us. They returned to their work. In twenty minutes the timer dinged. Lamont picked up books and papers from the floor. Arranging everything very neatly on his desk, he picked up a pencil and began writing. In five minutes he had finished a perfect paper!

A great smile, pride of achievement and a sense of being in charge radiated from him. Act of will. Inner authority. Self-esteem.

Once the concept is understood by the child and the parent or teacher's skill and sense of purpose has developed, it moves easily. It takes much less energy than the old authoritarian way. Both adult and child are winners.

"HE'S ELECTROCUTIN' ME!"

"Make Alvin stop electrocutin' me! It hurts!"

We were at the museum. The nylon carpeting caused the children to give each other a shock everytime they touched each other. Alvin delighted in doing it to everyone long after it ceased to be exciting.

Alvin was a student with many difficult problems. At times he would crawl on the floor of the classroom, hiding under the desks, staring out at everyone, refusing to respond. At the museum I said to him that it seemed as though his teaser subpersonality was working overtime. I then reminded him that he was in charge of himself. If he continued letting "The Tease" bother everyone, it would get him some burdens. I suggested that he might tell the subpersonality that it could tease some other time, when it was more appropriate. Once again I said, "You are in charge. It is your choice. Think it over and let me know what you decide."

A few moments later he came up to me and said, "I told it I didn't want no burdens. It's gone." He joined the group and didn't "electrocute" anyone else.

CAUTION:

Give questions and directions in a quiet, accepting voice. Be as objective as possible, *withholding all judgement*. Speak from center and not through one of your own subpersonalities.

One day I got very angry at the class and slammed a book down hard on the table for attention. After some angry words of demand and judgement, I took a deep breath and said, "You know, I, too, have a subpersonality that gets angry and has a temper. I look forward to the time when she no longer has to get so angry." The class laughed delightedly. One child said, "Yeah, I have one too!"

Communication — Sharing — Acceptance. We grow together.

UGLY DUCKLING

AREA: Self-esteem, self-awareness and subpersonalities.

COMMENT: An exercise designed to call forth the awareness of the potential of the individual. The child has the opportunity to become aware of his response to different types of personalities.

MEDIA: Hans Christian Andersen's *The Ugly Duckling*, total class discussion, simple drama, materials for puppet making, (paper sacks, paper plates, popsicle sticks, yarn, crayon, glue, scissors, etc.), pencils and paper. This unit takes several sessions spaced over one or two weeks.

PROCEDURE: Read the story, *The Ugly Duckling* by Hans Christian Andersen to the children, using one with good illustrations.

Have the children discuss the story, sharing parts they liked pest, parts they liked least and why.

Following the discussion ask them, "If you playacted it, what parts would you like to be?" Give every child a part. There can be many barnyard animals, several hunters, lots of geese, etc. If several want to be the ugly duckling they may draw names, vote or use some other creative way of choosing.

The acting is done very simply. Push the desks back to provide a large space. The children sit in a large circle on the floor. It is done primarily with just imagination and movement. No costumes or memorizing of lines are needed. Begin the first scene by having the mother duck crouched down with the baby ducks and ugly duckling nestled around her, pretending to be eggs. Read the introduction to the story and when the mother duck says something, simply read the part and let the child repeat it and act it out. Continue moving from scene to scene in this way. It is a very informal style similar to role playing.

It is a long story and is easily divided into two or three sessions.

Have the children discuss how they felt being the part they chose. Some questions that might be asked are: "How did you *feel* about the part you played?" "If you could choose another part what would it be?" "Which part would you like least?" "Why?" "Which part would you most like to be?" "Why?" "In real life are you ever like any of these parts?" "Which ones?" "When do you feel like an ugly duckling?" "When do you feel like a swan?"

Following the discussion you may have a language lesson and have them write about their feelings or respond to some of the questions.

An excellent art project to further increase the child's awareness is making puppets, followed by having the children tell the story with the puppets. Inviting others in to see it makes a grand finale.

OBSERVATION: Children's responses:

1. "I feel like an ugly duckling when. . ."
   "I feel like a ugly duckling when I am all alone."
   "I did not like my part because I know how people feel when they are called names."
   "I feel like a ugly duckling all the time."
   "I feel like a ugly duckling when I get beat up by my aunt."
   "A ugly duckling cutmuatapes (communicates) a whole way different then a swan cutmuatapes."
   "I wouldn't know if I would be a swan but I will know I was an ugly duckling."

2. "I feel like a beautiful swan when. . ."
   "I feel like a beautiful swan when my family is happy."
   "I feel like a beautiful swan when I have someone to be friends with."
   "I feel like a beautiful swan when I be realy quiet."
   "I feel like a beautiful swan when I'm wanted."

"When I was playing my part and all the thing that I was saying to Karen she might thing I am a duckling who though I was ugly. Karen was a ugly duck I didn't believe it that she was a beautiful duck."

"When I had to gather around Karen I felt silly."

Karen was indeed an "ugly duckling." She was tall, gangly, poorly coordinated, scattered and had great difficulty in relating to the rest of the children. Most of the time they treated her as the "ugly duckling." However, Karen had a creative imagination and a gift for acting. When the class was choosing parts they all wanted Karen to be the ugly duckling. Karen was delighted. Though the children believed Karen was the ugly duckling, Karen remembered what they had forgotten — that she would become the beautiful swan. Karen threw herself into the part of the ugly duckling with all her dramatic ability. When she unfolded into the beautiful swan she became suddenly graceful and very lovely. For a moment she had indeed become the beautiful swan.

I feel like a beautiful swan when I have someone to be friend with

when I feel like a ugly duku ducking when someone hits me.
I feel like a beautiful swan when I'm wanted

H.B.

Next time I whant to be a gose or a swan or a ugly duckling. I feel like an ugly duckling when I get mad. I feel like a beautiful swan when I be realy quiet.

5

Academic Achievement

SCANNING PROCESS
Preparation For Tests

AREA: Self-esteem, visualization, dis-identification, subpersonalities, Higher Self. Choice, self-correction, act of will. Releases energy for self-actualization.

COMMENT: This exercise is to be used only after children have had a thorough introduction to the concepts of attitudes, feelings, guided imagery, subpersonalities and the Wise Part within. It is especially good for relieving test anxiety. It can be used as a preparation for any activity for which the child may have anxiety or a special concern.

MEDIA: Class discussions, guided imagery. Test materials, pencil, paper.

PROCEDURE: Preparation and Visualization Process.
Preparation. Have several discussions to share general and individual concerns regarding tests.
1. Discuss: Why do we have tests? What other ways can we evaluate our progress? What are the benefits of testing? The burdens of testing? If you had your "druthers" what would you choose?
    Children become quite creative in their responses.
2. Discuss: What feelings do you have when taking tests? Evoke a list of both negative and positive feelings. The teacher may share some of his/her feelings and experiences of tests. Be personal — "I remember when. . . I felt. . ." Have each child share one feeling she/he has when taking a test.
    "I feel scared."
    "I feel nervous."
    "I feel dumb."
3. Discuss: What happens to your body when you take a test? *Where* in your body do you feel scared or nervous?
    "My hands feel sweaty."
    "I get a stomach ache."
    "My head hurts."
    "My heart beats real fast."
    "My mind goes blank and I can't remember anything."
    "My chest hurts."

This brings an awareness that they aren't alone or odd or different. Often the children are quite surprised that others feel the same, e.g. "You do too!" Such a discovery can transform a negative energy to a positive energy.

Visualization Process: Introduce this part of the exercise by saying something to the effect that: "We have been working hard in preparing for the big tests we will be taking next week. Today we're going to do something fun that will help you with the test. Believe it or not, it'll help you feel good about the tests! We are going to use our imaginations and do some immagery, so get yourself comfortable." By now the children know how to sit with feet on floor, hands quietly in lap or on desks, back straight, eyes closed.

Follow the alignment and breathing procedure used in Preparation For Guided Imagery. When the students are quietly receptive, say something to the following effect:

"Using that creative part of your mind, imagine or visualize yourself sitting at your desk with the test in front of you. See yourself sitting there feeling very comfortable. Your body feels just right. It feels rested and ready to work. It has lots of energy. The part of your body that gets scared during a test is comfortable and relaxed. See you body in perfect harmony. Your lungs, heart, stomach. . .all the parts of the body are healthy and feeling good.

Now see your emotions in perfect harmony. You feel calm and peaceful. All feelings of being scared or anxious are gone. You feel calm and peaceful. You feel confident, very capable. You feel good because you know you are able to do the work. You feel comfortable with yourself. See yourself sitting there in complete harmony with self-confidence and understanding.

Now see your mind working in complete harmony. That part of your mind that knows how to do math is alert. The part of the mind that knows how to add and when to carry, the part that knows how to subtract and when to borrow, the part that knows the timetables is in complete harmony and working well. Tell that part of you that likes to just sit and watch other people that it may watch people later. Tell that part of you that wants to play that it may play at recess. Tell the part that wants to daydream and look out the window, that it may daydream later. See yourself sitting there, at your desk, working on the test, feeling comfortable and knowing how to do it. You are capable. See yourself smiling, feeling good.

Continue sitting there and just experience that feeling of harmony, of being capable, relaxed and alert. Contact the Wise Part within you, and know what is right for you. . . When you are ready, in your own time, slowly return your thoughts to the room and open your eyes.

You may like to try this tonight after you have gone to bed. When the lights have been turned off and you have pulled the covers up, take a few moments before you go to sleep and visualize yourself taking the test in complete harmony, with that part of your mind that knows math, that knows reading, working perfectly for you. Your body feels good and your attitude is one of cooperation and confidence. Or you may wish to do it when you first wake up in the morning. Try it for the next few days and see what happens. It'll work. I know, because I've tried it for myself!"

Note: Do this slowly, giving time to visualize, to make choices, to experience the quietness.

OBSERVATION: The children were fascinated with this! In a class of 30 about 16 tried it the first night. Some said they forgot at night but remembered to do it in the morning. The scanning process scans, selects and visualizes the attitude to be held for the given task. It was done again in class for two days before the state testing. It was done again the morning of the test, after the tests had been passed to the students. Scanning was done before each test — math, reading and language. The teacher and assistant were amazed at how quietly and intensely the students worked with almost perfect concentration. Instructions had to be given only once. What a difference from the testing at the beginning of the year when the children were restless: some worked too fast just to get through, some refused to do it; instructions had to be repeated several times and extreme anxiety prevailed.

After each break the children returned to the room actually eager to continue with the test! Before each test section a brief Scanning Process and Preparation For Guided Imagery was done, allowing children to set aside anything that had happened at recess with the knowledge it would be dealt with later.

The scores were outstanding. There were, of course, many other factors involved. However, it is believed that the scanning technique had a major influence on the children's attitudes, helping to release the freedom to work at their full potential.

This was a Compensatory Education class of 28 black and 2 Native American fourth grade students in an inner-city elementary school in the Bay Area of northern California. The children in a Compensatory Education program are below the 50th percentile, or two or more years below grade level. The growth in reading from October to May ranged from the highest of 3.7 (growth of three years plus seven months) to the lowest of .5. The .5 score was the growth of a child who had been recommended for an EH class (Educable Handicapped). She had an extremely short attention span. When she was five years old she got into the refrigerator and ate a sugar cube with LSD. In previous testing she had simply refused to work or would just put marks on the paper in order to relieve the tension. Following the Scanning Process she worked very hard on the test and was able to show a reading score of 5 months' growth.

Not only does the Scanning Process release the child to work at potential, but it transforms the usual test anxiety syndrome to a harmonious individual and group experience. Encouraging this experience was the fact that I did a Scanning Process in visualizing myself administering the test harmoniously and with serenity and confidence.

The project involved treatment and control groups for the psychosynthesis approach as presented here. Criteria for evaluation included the Piers-Harris Children's Self-Concept Inventory and the Comprehensive Test of Basic Skills (CTBS). See Appendix for project results.

Two years following the project my own skills in the application of the principles and techniques of psychosynthesis had advanced to such a degree that I was using them daily in all areas of the classroom. The CTBS reading scores of this year's fifth graders (same inner-city school) were outstanding. The class average in the fall CTBS testing was 2.4 (second grade, four months). The spring CTBS class average in reading was 6.0 (sixth grade), an average growth of 4.6 (four years, six months). This class had the highest reading average of all the SB-90 schools in the district.

FOURTH GRADE TEST SCORES

		Reading			Math	
Name	Oct	May	Growth	Oct	May	Growth
1. Doris*	7.0	9.7	2.7	5.9	7.5	1.6
2. Joyce	5.6	7.0	1.4	4.5	5.4	.9
3. Kathy	3.5	4.8	1.3	3.1	4.6	1.5
4. Gael	2.8	3.8	1.0	3.5	4.2	.7
5. Anne	1.7	2.2	.5	2.2	2.3	.1 (EH)
6. Rose	3.2	3.9	.7	3.7	4.5	.8
7. Cheryl	3.7	6.1	2.4	3.9	5.1	1.2
8. Carol	4.3	7.0	2.7	3.2	3.9	.9
9. Karen		2.5			3.7	
10. Patty	3.8	4.3	1.5	3.2	4.3	1.1
11. Marie	3.0	7.7	3.0	5.4	6.5	1.1
12. Sue	3.7	5.4	1.7	3.2	4.8	1.6
13. Ruth	4.1	6.1	2.0	3.8	5.2	1.4
14. Betty	2.0	3.2	1.2	3.5	4.2	.7
15. Tim	2.2	3.2	1.0	2.6	3.7	.9
16. Joe	3.1	4.7	1.6	3.2	4.5	1.3
17. Tom	4.7	7.3	2.6	3.7	5.6	1.9
18. John	2.9	3.9	1.0	2.9	4.3	2.6
19. Jerry	3.3	7.0	3.7	4.1	6.2	2.1
20. Dick	2.1	2.9	.8	2.4	3.2	.8
21. Jose	3.7	5.1	1.4	3.0	4.1	1.1
22. Lito	1.9	3.8	1.9	2.9	3.5	.6
23. Eric	3.0	3.5	.5	2.4	2.7	.3
24. Gus	3.0	3.9	.9	3.2	4.9	1.7
25. Bob	3.5	5.6	1.9	3.6	5.7	2.1
26. Bill	3.4	3.9	.5	4.2	5.4	1.2
27. Jim	3.8	7.3	3.5	5.0	6.5	1.5
28. Don		3.2			3.6	

*Names have been changed.

Note: These are scores for the class that experienced the initial Scanning Process reported above. The following year a project using psychosynthesis in the classroom was initiated as a part of a research program for a Master's Degree.

There is a need to share here that other than the psychosynthesis approach of what I have come to call the "4th R" - reading, 'riting, 'rithmetic and right relations, I used a traditional teaching program of basic skills or basic onesies and twosies. It must be emphasized that we are to teach for a balance of both academic and personal relations skills if children are to be supported in experiencing their full personhood. I must continually stress that education means *educare* — to *call forth*.

6

Death

DEATH
"Teacher! Myrtle the Turtle Is Dead!"

"Teacher! Myrtle the Turtle is dead!" These words greeted me as I arrived in my fourth grade class one morning. "Oh dear," I thought, "Now what do I do?"

Myrtle the Turtle was a classroom pet. Harold had brought him with pride and shared him shyly and lovingly with the class. The children had fed him, talked about him and watched him dreamily when needing to retreat for awhile.

Just the day before one of the reading groups had been reading about the death of a turtle. The children in the story had a funeral for it. It had stimulated quite a discussion about pets.

Now Myrtle the Turtle was dead. The children asked if they could have a funeral.

"Yes," I heard myself answering. "We can have a funeral."

"When?"

"After lunch."

Inwardly I thought, "What if the principal comes in? How do I handle this?" I believed, though, in the importance of allowing children to experience grief, to express it and experience release and healing.

When I returned from lunch the children were already in the classroom. Some of the girls had gone home and brought flowers. Some of the boys had fashioned a small box out of paper and much tape. I saw that much talking and planning had gone on during lunch.

Edward said, "I'll be the pallbearer. I know what to do."

Edward's father had died suddenly of a heart attack in October and it was now April. He was an only child, very close to his father. Edward had been crying almost daily since then.

I was hesitant. . . "But. . . Yes," I thought, "let him experience it. Perhaps healing will come."

The children all agreed that Edward was to do it. Desks were pushed back. A table was placed in front of the room. The flowers were placed on the table. Edward went to the back of the room and announced that he would carry the coffin and the rest were to sing as he marched in. I was stunned to hear the children immediately begin chanting a funeral dirge in total rhythm. Where had they learned it?

As Edward placed the "coffin" by the flowers the children said to me, "Now you've got to say a prayer! You've got to be the minister!" "Oh my," I said to myself," I think this is supposed to be against the law!" However, I did say a couple of sentences, giving thanks for the happiness we had had with Myrtle the Turtle. The children took it all very seriously, with occasional giggles of excitement and nervousness.

A spontaneous sharing began. The children shared about funerals they had attended, asking and giving answers to each other. One girl shared about how her cousin, a Black Panther, was killed in a shootout and how her aunt had thrown herself on the coffin. Another shared about her uncle being killed in a motorcycle accident. One shared about how a neighbor got mad and killed his wife and the family all went to the funeral. They talked about the music, about things the minister said, about the behavior of the people. I was surprised at how much these children had experienced about death. They learned that there were different types of funerals. I shared that funerals were a way people expressed their love as well as their grief. However, mostly I just sat and listened to their sharing with a minimum of direction.

Edward shared a little about his father's funeral. The class listened intently and lovingly every time a child shared. A sense of caring and acceptance for each other was present. Edward rarely cried the rest of the year. He began playing and laughing more. Something seemed to be released within him that day.

The use of drama, the creative imagination and an opportunity to share in a loving and accepting environment are surely all a part of the process of expanding the awareness of self, of acceptance of self and self-esteem.

AREA: Self-esteem, self-awareness, self-healing.

COMMENT: This is designed to help the child become aware of death as a part of life. Often the subject of death is confusing and frightening for children. A nine-year-old child generally has had some experience of death; the death of a pet, a grandparent, a neighbor, a close friend. Exposure to death by television is a routine happening but lacks personal involvement.

When the child has experienced discussing the subject of death in a comfortable way another bit of awareness about himself has taken place. The awareness that he can handle the subject without fear adds to his self-esteem.

MEDIA: Large and small group discussion, available books (see Bibliography).

PROCEDURE: Books on death need to be available in the home, classroom, or school library. Trust the child's inner self to guide him in the selection. When the child picks up the book and is ready to handle the subject he will check it out; if he is not ready, he will put it down.

Joanne Bernstein of Brooklyn College has developed an extensive bibliography on death and suicide in *Children's Literature*, which is included in the Bibliography at the end of this handbook. In a workshop at the International Reading Convention in 1976, Bernstein reported on a statistical analysis of the image of death and suicide in contemporary children's literature for three five-year periods in order to note trends. She said, "It appears that the taboo on discussion of death is slowly lifting."

A Taste of Blackberries by Doris R. Smith (New York: T. Y. Crowell and Co., 1973) is a beautiful story to read to children. It offers an opportunity for sharing of feelings and experiences on death. It is about a young boy whose friend dies from a bee sting. In a very simple and loving way it deals with the boy's feelings of grief and loss.

CAUTION: Only the adult who is comfortable with his/her own feelings about death should attempt such discussions. Feelings are contagious. If it is not comfortable for you, do not feel you have to discuss it.

OBSERVATION: Generally children are quite curious about death. They are eager to talk about it. One day as I returned to class after attending a funeral a child asked, "Did you cry?" Another child said, "Don't ask that! It isn't nice."

I replied, "That's all right. Yes, I did cry. You know, there are many types of tears. Tears of sadness, tears of joy, tears of pain. My aunt died. I loved her very much, and I shall miss her. Mine were tears of sadness."

This triggered a lengthy and exciting discussion on death and tears. There was no judging of right or wrong, but simple sharing of feelings. The children's awareness had expanded to include acceptance of tears as a natural part of life.

Appendix

The project in which the activities described in this book were developed began in the spring of 1976 in an inner-city class of 32 fourth graders — 17 boys and 16 girls. Of these, 29 were black, two were Native American, and one was Caucasian. Economically, they were lower middle class, with many on welfare. Because their reading, math, and language scores on the Comprehensive Test of Basic Skills were below the 50th percentile, and twenty-seven of the thirty-two children scored two or more years below grade level, they were part of the Compensatory Education program funded by California's Senate Bill 90. Not only were they low academically but they also were extremely unadaptive in behavior and poor in attitude. They had severe behavioral problems and were almost totally dependent on external control, without any concept or recognition of self-control or responsibility for their own behavior.

In September, 1976, the activities were begun with a combination class of 31 fourth and fifth graders. Again, because of their low test scores, these children were in the Compensatory Education program. A class of 32 fourth-graders who had no contact with the treatment group was selected as a control group.

The Piers-Harris Self-Concept Scale[1] was given in November as a pretest to both groups. A post-test was given in March to determine whether there was a measurable difference between the groups in self-esteem as well as in observable behavior.

The Piers-Harris Self-Concept Scale entitled "The Way I Feel About Myself" is a quickly completed (15-20 minutes) self-report instrument designed for children in a wide age range. Administered in a group setting, it requires approximately a third-grade reading knowledge. On an individual basis it might be used below that level.

Developed in 1965, the standardized test consists of 80 statements requiring "yes" or "no" answers. Some of the statements are "My classmates make fun of me," "I am a happy person," and "My parents expect too much of me." Categories covered are (1) physical characteristics and appearance; (2) home and family; (3) ability in sports; (4) ability in school, attitudes toward school, etc.; (5) intellectual abilities; (6) just me, myself; and (7) personality, character, inner resources, and emotional tendencies.

The data assessing increases in self-concept were analyzed statistically in order to answer the following questions:

(1) Did the treatment group outperform the control group on the Piers-Harris test?

(2) Were there significant differences from pre-test to post-test for the treatment and control groups?

(3) For the treatment group, was there a significant difference between the fourth and fifth graders?

(4) For the treatment group, were there significant differences between males and females?

In general, the treatment group responded favorably to the project activities in terms of their self-concept as measured by the Piers-Harris Scale. They made a significant gain from pre-test to post-test, whereas the control group made no significant gain during the same period. There were no mean score differences between the groups on the pre-test, the post-test, or the gain score in self-concept. There also were no significant mean differences between fourth and fifth graders or between males and females, although fourth graders and females scored slightly lower.

To determine whether there were significant differences between the treatment and control groups in reading scores from pre-test to post-test, the Comprehensive Test of Basic Skills (CTBS) results were used. The treatment group had a mean growth of one year, nine months in reading, while the control group had a mean growth of almost nine months, a difference of over one year in a period of five teaching months.

Because of the transience of the school population, only 17 or the original 32 students in the treatment group and 18 of the original 32 students in the control group remained at the time of the CTBS post-test.

The Piers-Harris Scale was developed primarily for research. Doctors Ellen Piers and Dale Harris are of the opinion that self-attitudes are relatively stable, although probably less so in childhood than in adolescence. This means that studies which attempt to measure change after a single laboratory event, according to Piers-Harris, may not find significant differences. Longer term studies are, therefore, recommended. These authors also state that it is unwise to assume that any special groups will necessarily show differences in mean self-concept.

It is their impression that with children, young children in particular, the desire to "look good" is fairly strong. Rather than reflecting a deliberate attempt to mislead, their responses may frequently reflect a confusion between how they really feel or act and how they have been told they should feel and act. If this is so, then getting an accurate or "true" response on self-esteem would be difficult.

Considering the observable behavior of the two groups, the Piers-Harris scores were higher than expected. A possible explanation for this difference is the theory that there may be an exterior, exaggerated sense of self-worth in children who have been deprived of self-esteem building experiences such as the children involved in the project. An inflated or incipient self-esteem may be acquired as a survival response due to painful life experiences.

Many of these children had been involved in traumatic experiences. One boy had been in so many foster homes that he was disturbed enough to crawl on the floor among the desks and along the walls so as not to be seen and was filled with much hostility and confusion.

Both treatment and control groups shared such life experiences. It must be remembered, however, that there were also many parents who were doing their best to raise their children in loving, supportive homes. Therefore, the observable behavior in classroom, playground, lunch room and at all school gatherings may serve well as measures of assessment, especially for assessing self-discipline as well as self-esteem.

The control group had an unexpectedly difficult year. After school had been in session for two months in the fall, a new class of fourth graders was created from three different classes in order to relieve the overcrowded classrooms. The new teacher for this class was a former principal who had not been in the classroom for twenty-three years. He worked very hard with the children and often talked in the faculty lunch room about the near total lack of self-discipline of the children. In three months he was transferred and, for the rest of the year, the class had a series of substitutes.

The control group's observable behavior on the playground, in the lunch room, at assemblies, etc. became increasingly poor, with fights, disregard for general school rules such as bells and use of play equipment, etc. In general, children were aggressive and noncooperative; one teacher called them the "orphaned" class. The situation made the responses to the Piers-Harris Self-Concept Scale most interesting since children in this group indicated they had high self-esteem. This discrepancy points to the need for more research on the relationship between self reported self-esteem and self-discipline observed in behavior.

The treatment group differed only in that it remained in a stable classroom environment with one teacher for the year and experienced the various activities and exercises developed in the project.

Even though there was significant gain in the treatment group's Piers-Harris Scale scores, it is perhaps through the observable behavior that the greatest gain from the treatment can be recognized. At the beginning of the school year, the researcher felt that it probably was the most difficult class she had experienced in all her years of teaching. It was due partly to this difficulty that the decision was made to do intensive work with the children in developing awareness of attitudes, choice, and responsibility of action through the use of the self-esteem building activities.

By the end of the school year, the class was displaying notable changes in observable behaviors. They were working independently and cooperatively. They were able to work in small groups and give each other help. The fights, arguments, foul language and poor work habits were far less noticeable, and children demonstrated the awareness of the use of self-discipline with a sense of achievement. Their academic scores made a considerable increase which can be seen in the exercise on Scanning, page 85.

All of this evidence lends support to the strength of the project and encourages the continued use of the activities based on principles of psychosynthesis as a means for developing self-esteem and inner control. The control group's lesser gain in self-concept during this period indicates the need for such a program.

LIMITATIONS OF THE PROJECT

The change of the treatment class from a straight fourth grade class in the spring to a combination class of fifth and fourth graders in the fall changed the effectiveness of the program. The demands of planning for and teaching a class of two grades severely limited the time available for implementing the project as extensively as desired. During the first semester of the project, when the exercises were presented to a straight fourth grade class, more time was available and the observable response was better.

The late decision to administer the Piers-Harris Self-Concept Scale may have limited the results. Having the control group within the same school with all of the unexpected problems may also have confounded the results.

SPECIFIC RECOMMENDATIONS FOR FURTHER STUDY

1. Administer the Piers-Harris Self-Concept Scale to both treatment and control groups within the first two weeks of school as opposed to later. In this project, it was not given until November, almost three months into the school year, when the treatment group had already received much work in psychosynthesis processes.

2. If at all possible, the control group should be as stable as the treatment group. It would be interesting to have the control group in another school with a similar student population to examine the extent to which children and teachers in the same school influence each other.

3. Implement the project in a suburban school and compare results to those of the project administered in an inner-city school. While the findings of this project indicated no difference between grade levels or sex, it would be interesting to note if there is a difference in response due to economic or cultural background.

4. Ensure that both treatment and control groups have the same teacher since a difference between the groups could be due to the personalities of different teachers.

RESPONSES TO THE ACTIVITIES

In addition to evaluating changes in children's behavior, the project evaluated the responses of teachers, psychosynthesists, and those having both teaching and psychosynthesis training to the concepts and techniques used in the project. Responses to an evaluation questionnaire were analyzed statistically to determine whether the responses of these professionals to various aspects of the project were significantly more positive than negative.

The response of all three groups was found to be very positive, indicating that the approach is on a firm basis both pedagogically and psychologically. Some comments were:

"What a fantastic tool to help children grow emotionally."
—Ph.D., Psychologist-Counselor

"I appreciate that most of these exercises flow from the child's inner focus of control; there is so much inner wisdom and strength that can be evoked from kids."
—B.S., Psychology

"You are offering a service I see as greatly needed by our society in its present state."
—Ph.D., Psychologist-Teacher

"Please do more! Excellent and valuable for all children!"
—M.S.W., Social Worker

"Many of the exercises could be translated into simple directives for parents. . . Excellent to correlate school and home. . ."
—Speech Pathologist

"The entire theme is positive. . .I would like to try some of the exercises!"
—Second-grade Teacher (42 years' teaching experience!)

Parents, also, responded very positively to the activities being done in their children's classroom. At one parent conference, a mother said, "Well, I've certainly been wondering what's been happening. He's changed so much [in self-esteem]." Another said, "What's this about goals? Tacelia does her homework as soon as she gets home. She says she's winning her goal!" One parent even went so far as to insist very strongly that the principal move her daughter into the treatment class. Still another parent stated, "I have eight children, and I wish I'd had this when they were growing up!"

The parents were pleased not only with the behavioral changes in their children but also with the academic achievements on the CTBS.

GENERAL RECOMMENDATIONS

Developing a curriculum that includes both the affective and cognitive aspects of the student is still a new process. The value of the holistic approach to education is still questioned by some educators and more research is needed to support it.

Courses led by skilled teachers need to be available to other teachers. For best results, the teacher needs to be making continued growth in her own self-esteem and inner authority while working with the children in these areas.

It is strongly recommended that continued studies be made in the area of holistic education. A curriculum needs to be developed that presents a sequential growth pattern of personal awareness in relationship to the child's individual physical, emotional, mental, and spiritual growth. This curriculum, started in the primary grades, needs to be as much a part of the basic curriculum as reading and math. The traditional "3 R's" need to include a fourth "R," that of "Right Human Relations."

We must establish within school curricula the affective experiences that are such a necessary part of the child's growth. The child who grows in self-esteem and who has a sense of her/his inner authority is able to function as an integrated personality, contributing to life freely and joyously.

[1]For additional information regarding this test, please contact: Counselor Recordings and Tests; Box 6184; Acklen Station; Nashville, Tennessee. (For parents and teachers interested in such measures there are many other standardized tests available as well. I encourage you to work with a psychologist who specializes in testing, as lay use of clinical instruments may lead to mis-interpretations.)

Bibliography

Alschuler, Alfred. "Psychological Education," *Journal for Humanistic Psychology,* Spring 1969.

Anderson, Robert A., *Stress Power! How To Turn Tension Into Energy.* New York: Human Sciences Press, 1978.

Assagioli, Roberto. *Psychosynthesis.* New York: Viking Press, 1965.

_____. *The Act of Will.* New York: Viking Press, 1973.

_____. *Jung and Psychosynthesis.* P.F.R. Issue No. 19. New York: Psychosynthesis Research Foundation, 1970.

_____. Psychosynthesis and the Self. Mimeographed transcripts of the seminar for High Point Foundation Leaders in Capaplona, Italy, July, 1973.

_____. *The Balancing and Synthesis of the Opposites.* P.R.F. Issue No. 29. New York: Psychosynthesis Research Foundation, 1970.

_____. *The Technique of Evocative Words.* P.R.F. Issue No. 25. New York: Psychosynthesis Research Foundation, 1970.

Barron, Frank. *Creativity and Personal Freedom.* Princeton, New Jersey: D. Van Nostrand Company, Inc., 1968.

Birnbaum, Max. "Sense About Sensitivity Training," *Saturday Review,* November 15, 1969.

Brown, George I. "Affectivity, Classroom Climate, and Teaching." Washington, D.C.: *American Federation of Teachers,* 1971. EMS No.6.

_____. *Human Teaching For Human Learning: An Introduction to Confluent Education.* New York: Viking Press, 1971.

_____. *The Live Class Room: Innovation Through Confluent Education and Gestalt.* New York: Viking Press, 1975.

Canfield, Jack, and Harold C. Wells. *100 Ways to Enhance Self-Concept In The Classroom.* New Jersey: Prentice-Hall, Inc., 1976.

Coppersmith, S. *The Antecedents of Self-Esteem.* San Francisco: Freeman Press, 1967.

Cousins, Norman. *Anatomy of an Illness.* New York: W.W. Norton and Co., 1979.

Crary, Ryland E., *Humanizing the School: Curriculum Development and Theory.* Alfred A. Knopf, Inc., 1969.

DeMille, Richard. *Put Your Mother on the Ceiling.* New York: Viking Press, 1972.

Fantini, Mario D., and Gerald Weinstein. *Toward a Contract Curriculum.* New York: Harper & Row, 1968.

Ferrucci, Piero. *What We May Be.* Los Angeles: J.P. Tarcher, Inc. 1982.

Frankl, Viktor. *From Death Camp to Existentialism.* Boston: Beacon Press, 1959.

Freed, Alvyn M. *TA for Tots.* Sacramento, Calif.: Jalmar Press, Inc., 1973.

Glasser, William. *Schools Without Failure.* New York: Harper and Row, 1969.

Gordon, Thomas. *Parent Effectiveness Training.* New York: Peter Wyden, 1970.

_____. *Teacher Effectiveness Training.* New York: Peter Wyden, 1974.

Harman, W.W., "The New Copernican Revolution," *Stanford Today.* Winter 1959, p. 6, (J. G. Vargiu. *Global Education and Psychosynthesis.* Psychosynthesis Research Foundation, Inc., 1971.)

Hendricks, Gay and Russel Wills. *The Centering Book: awareness activities for children, parents, and teachers.* Englewood Cliffs, N.J.: Prentice-Hall, 1975.

Horowitz, Mark, and Marilyn Kriegel. "A Course in Psycho-Synthesis." *Psychosynthesis Institute News Calendar,* Vol. 5, No. 1, Spring 1975.

Huxley, Laura. *You Are Not the Target.* New York: Farrar, Strauss & Giroux, 1963.

Jones, Ron. "Take as Directed," *The CoEvolution Quarterly,* Sausalito, Ca., Spring 1976.

Koch, Kenneth. *Wishes, Lies and Dreams.* New York: Chelsea House (Random House), 1970.

Kohl, Herbert. *36 Children.* New York: The New American Library, 1967.

Maslow, Abraham H. *The Creative Attitude.* P.R.F. Reprint No. 10. New York: Psychosynthesis Research Foundation, 1963.

_____. *Motivation and Personality.* New York: Harper, 1970.

May, Rollo. *Love and Will.* New York: Norton, 1969.

Milhollen, Frank, and Bill E. Forisha. *From Skinner to Rogers: Contrasting Approaches to Education.* Professional Educators Publications, Inc., Nebraska, 1972.

Moustakas, Clark. *The Authentic Teacher.* Cambridge, Mass.: Howard A. Doyle Publishing Co., 1972.

Rainwater, Janette. *You're in Charge! A Guide to Becoming Your Own Therapist.* Los Angeles, Ca.: Guild of Tutors Press, 1979.

Raths, Louis E., Merrill Harmin, and Sidney B. Simon. *Values and Teaching.* Columbus, Ohio: Charles E. Merrill Publishing Co., 1966.

Rogers, Carl R. *Freedom to Learn.* Columbus, Ohio: Charles E. Merrill Publishing Co., 1969.

Rogers, C. R. and B. Stevens. *Person to Person: The Problem of Being Human.* Walnut Creek, Ca.: Real People Press, 1967.

Rubin, Louis J. *Facts and Feelings in the Classroom.* New York: Walker and Co., 1973.

Samples, Robert E. "Learning with the Whole Brain," *Human Behavior*, 1975.

Schofield, Harry. *The Philosophy of Education*. London: Allen and Unwin Ltd., 1972.

Silberman, Charles E. *Crisis in the Classroom*. New York: Random House, 1970.

Skinner, B. F. *Science and Human Behavior*. New York: Macmillan, 1953.

Steiner, Claude, *The Original Warm Fuzzy Tale*. Sacramento, Calif.: Jalmar Press, 1977.

Synthesis: The Realization of Self. Vol. 1, No. 1, Redwood City, Ca., 1974.

Tesconi, Charles, Jr., and Van Cleve Morris. *The Anti-Man Culture*. Chicago: University of Illinois Press, 1972.

Thoresen, Carl E. *Behavioral Humanism*. Research and Development Memorandum, Stanford University, Ca., 1972.

Van De Riet, Vernon, and Michael B. Resnick. *Learning to Learn, an Effective Model for Early Childhood Education*. Gainesville, Florida: University of Florida, 1973.

Vargiu, James G. *A Model of Creative Behavior*. Redwood City, Ca.: Psychosynthesis Institute, 1973.

_____. *Global Education and Psychosynthesis*. New York: Psychosynthesis Research Foundation, 1971.

Wann, T. W. *Behaviorism and Phenomenology, Contrasting Basis for Modern Psychology*. Chicago: University of Chicago Press, 1964.

Weinstein, Gerald, and Mario D. Fantini. *Toward Humanistic Education, A Curriculum of Affect*. New York: Praeger Publishers, 1970.

Bernstein, Joanne. *Loss.* Seabury, 1977. Age 10+.
A guide for young people who have lost someone close, touching upon both practical and emotional aspects of death and its aftermath.

Bernstein, Joanne and Stephen Gullo. *When People Die.* Dutton, 1976. 5-9.
Life, death, and loss are investigated from the perspective of one woman's death.

Corley, Elizabeth. *Tell Me About Death: Tell Me About Funerals.* Grammatical Sciences, 1973. 7-11.
This paperback provides a matter-of-fact yet reassuring explanation of funeral and burial procedures, as well as discussion of loss.

Grollman, Earl. *Talking About Death.* Beacon, 1971. 5+.
Intended as the parent's script for a dialogue to take place between parent and child, the author's words warmly open discussion.

Harris, Audrey. *Why Did He Die?* Lerner, 1965. 5-9.
Gentle rhyme serves to help one youngster cope with the death of a friend's grandfather.

Klein, Stanley. *The Final Mystery.* Doubleday, 1975. 8-13.
Comparative religious practices, the life cycle, and humanity's fight against death are the focal points of this cross-cultural study.

Langone, John. *Death Is a Noun.* Little, Brown, 1972. Dell, 1975. 12+.
Up-to-date research is the backbone of this readable examination of death's dilemma: medical death, facing death, euthanasia, suicide, etc.

LeShan, Eda. *What Makes Me Feel This Way?* Macmillan, 1972. 8+.
One beautiful chapter treats death and fear of dying.

Lifton, Robert Jay and Eric Olson. *Living and Dying.* Praeger, 1974. 14+.
Fascinating, scholarly, and intellectually demanding, this historical overview explores responses to death through the ages, concentrating most heavily upon the present nuclear age.

Segerberg, Jr. Osborn. *Living With Death.* Praeger, 1974. 14+.
Drawing from recent research, the author seeks to answer questions about death's mystery, the good death, and the good life which leads to it.

Smith, Doris R. *A Taste of Blackberries.* T. Y. Crowell & Co., 1973.
About a young boy whose friend dies from a bee sting.

Stein, Sarah. *About Dying.* Walker, 1974. 4-9.
One narrative, for children, tells of plant, animal, and human death, as well as reactions to death. The other, for parents, explains the psychodynamics of loss responses and urges honesty.

Turner, Ann. *Houses for the Dead: Burial Customs Through the Ages.* McKay, 1976. 12+.

Burial rites, mourning beliefs and practices, funeral customs, ghost myths, and superstitions are discussed across time and many cultures.

Zim, Herbert and Sonia Bleeker. *Life and Death.* Morrow, 1970. 8-12.

The first nonfiction book about death for children, this book presents a calm, scientific explanation of the cycle of life and death. Customs around the world and comparative beliefs are also part of the book, which remains a classic in its field.

THE CREATIVE PARENTING/CREATIVE TEACHING SERIES FROM JALMAR PRESS

The Creative Parenting/Creative Teaching Series presents an array of practical purposeful materials to help you in your job as a parent or other caring adult working with children. Parents are playing an increasingly vital role in their children's educations; teachers look for ways to effectively incorporate and assist parents' efforts at home as well as at school. Counselors, health practitioners, and educational specialists, too, look for useful materials that help them relate better to families and children.

Jalmar's Creative Parenting/Creative Teaching Series provides the support materials for all adult endeavors to enhance children's lives in meaningful and creative ways.

Books in Jalmar's Creative Parenting/Creative Teaching Series

UNICORNS ARE REAL: A RIGHT-BRAINED APPROACH TO LEARNING
by Barbara Meister Vitale

An illustrated activity book showing parents and teachers how to tap into children's "right-brained" strengths (using color, imagery, touch, sound, and movement) to teach "left-brain" school tasks.

$9.95 Trade Paperback — 150 pages

CHARLES THE CLOWN'S GUIDE TO CHILDREN'S PARTIES
by Charles and Linda Kraus

A resource book of helpful party guidelines plus age-appropriate activities that naturally motivate and absorb children. Helps you to learn about all children as well as plan for that special event!

$9.95 Illustrated Trade Paperback — 320 pages

"HE HIT ME BACK FIRST!" CREATIVE VISUALIZATION ACTIVITIES FOR TEACHING & PARENTING
by Eva D. Fugitt

Based on psychosynthesis, this activity book lovingly guides children to self-correcting behavior. Children become aware of choice and their "Wise Part" within which helps them choose appropriate behaviors in all their interactions.

$9.95 Trade Paperback — 116 pages

PITCHING IN: HOW TO TEACH YOUR CHILDREN TO WORK AROUND THE HOUSE
by Charles Spellman and Rachel Williams

Adults who worked around the house as children are more successful later in life, research shows. Here's a simple system plus sound parenting advice and humor, too!

$5.45 Illustrated Trade Paperback — 102 pages

THE PARENT BOOK: THE HOLISTIC PROGRAM FOR RAISING THE EMOTIONALLY MATURE CHILD
by Harold Bessell and Thomas P. Kelly Jr.

A child-raising guide for children ages 3-14 that tells you how to live with your children in a way that encourages their healthy emotional development.

FIRST TIME OUT: SKILLS FOR LIVING AWAY FROM HOME
by Reva Camiel and Hila Michaelsen

A positive, comprehensive guide for young adults leaving home for the first time. Helps turn a hazardous time for parents and teens into a constructive and satisfying adventure for all.

$5.95 Trade Paperback — 220 pages

PAJAMAS DON'T MATTER (OR WHAT YOUR BABY REALLY NEEDS)
by Trish Gribben, Illustrated by Dick Frizzell

Valuable information and needed reassurances to new parents as they struggle through the frantic, but rewarding, first years of their child's life.

$5.95 Illustrated Trade Paperback — 52 pages

Write to Jalmar Press for free catalog describing these and other teaching materials for the handicapped and the gifted, as well as our full line of Transactional Analysis products for all ages:

JALMAR PRESS - 45 Hitching Post Drive — Rolling Hills Estates, CA 90274